Cakes
WINNING RECIPES

Publications International, Ltd.
Favorite Brand Name Recipes at www.fbnr.com

Pictured on the front cover *(left to right):* Cookies 'n' Cream Cake *(page 60),* Chocolate Hazelnut Cupcake *(page 106),* Chocolate Almond Torte *(page 84),* Chocolate-Covered Coconut Almond Cake *(page 92),* New York Cheesecake *(page 138),* Chocolate Vanilla Swirl Cheesecake *(page 128),* Red Velvet Cupcake *(page 114)* and European Mocha Fudge Cake *(page 34).*
Pictured on the back cover *(top to bottom):* Espresso Chocolate Cheesecake *(page 136)* and Blueberry Crumb Cake *(page 58).*

ISBN-13: 978-1-4127-9792-4
ISBN-10: 1-4127-9792-6

Library of Congress Control Number: 2009920388

Manufactured in China.

8 7 6 5 4 3 2 1

Microwave Cooking: Microwave ovens vary in wattage. Use the cooking times as guidelines and check for doneness before adding more time.

Preparation/Cooking Times: Preparation times are based on the approximate amount of time required to assemble the recipe before cooking, baking, chilling or serving. These times include preparation steps such as measuring, chopping and mixing. The fact that some preparations and cooking can be done simultaneously is taken into account. Preparation of optional ingredients and serving suggestions is not included.

Table of Contents

The Classics

Butterscotch Bundt Cake

1 package (about 18 ounces) yellow cake mix *without* pudding
   in the mix
1 package (4-serving size) butterscotch instant pudding and
   pie filling mix
1 cup water
3 eggs
2 teaspoons ground cinnamon
½ cup chopped pecans
   Powdered sugar (optional)

1. Preheat oven to 325°F. Spray 12-cup bundt pan with nonstick cooking spray.

2. Beat cake mix, pudding mix, water, eggs and cinnamon in large bowl with electric mixer at medium-high speed 2 minutes or until blended. Stir in pecans. Pour batter into prepared pan.

3. Bake 40 to 50 minutes or until cake springs back when lightly touched. Cool cake in pan 10 minutes; invert cake onto serving plate to cool completely. Sprinkle with powdered sugar.   *Makes 12 to 16 servings*

Pistachio Walnut Bundt Cake: Substitute white cake mix for yellow cake mix, pistachio pudding mix for butterscotch pudding and walnuts for pecans.

Moist and Tender Carrot Cake

2 cups granulated sugar
1½ cups vegetable oil
1 teaspoon vanilla
2½ cups all-purpose flour
1 tablespoon plus 1 teaspoon ground cinnamon, divided
1 teaspoon salt
1 teaspoon baking soda
½ teaspoon ground ginger
4 eggs
2 cups grated carrots
1 cup canned crushed pineapple, drained and juice reserved
¾ cup chopped pecans
½ cup golden raisins
Pineapple juice
Cream Cheese Frosting (recipe follows)

1. Preheat oven to 350°F. Grease and flour two 8-inch round cake pans. Combine sugar, oil and vanilla in large bowl. Sift flour, 1 tablespoon cinnamon, salt, baking soda and ginger into medium bowl; add to sugar mixture alternately with eggs, mixing well after each addition. Stir in carrots, pineapple, pecans and raisins until well blended. Pour into prepared pans.

2. Bake 45 to 50 minutes or until toothpick inserted into centers comes out clean. Poke holes in warm layers with wooden skewer. Combine reserved pineapple juice with enough additional juice to equal 2 cups. Pour 1 cup over each layer. Let layers stand until cool and juice is absorbed.

3. Prepare Cream Cheese Frosting. Invert one cake layer onto serving plate; spread with frosting. Place second layer over frosting. Frost top and side of cake; sprinkle with remaining 1 teaspoon cinnamon. Store cake in refrigerator. *Makes 10 to 12 servings*

Cream Cheese Frosting: Beat 2 cups (4 sticks) softened butter, 1 package (8 ounces) softened cream cheese and 2 tablespoons vanilla in large bowl with electric mixer until light and fluffy. Stir in 2 cups powdered sugar until blended. If frosting is too thick, stir in whipping cream, 1 tablespoon at a time, until desired consistency is reached.

Moist and Tender Carrot Cake

Lemon Chiffon Cake

1½ cups cake flour
2½ teaspoons baking powder
⅛ teaspoon salt
1 cup plus 2 tablespoons granulated sugar, divided
¼ cup plus 2 tablespoons buttermilk
¼ cup canola oil
¼ cup lemon juice
2 egg yolks
Grated peel of 1 lemon
1 teaspoon vanilla
6 egg whites, at room temperature
½ teaspoon cream of tartar
2 teaspoons powdered sugar (optional)

1. Preheat oven to 325°F. Sift flour, baking powder and salt into medium bowl. Stir in 1 cup granulated sugar until blended.

2. Beat buttermilk, oil, lemon juice, egg yolks, lemon peel and vanilla in large bowl with electric mixer at medium speed 1 minute or until smooth. Gradually beat in flour mixture at low speed until blended. Beat at medium speed 30 seconds or until smooth.

3. Beat egg whites and cream of tartar in separate large bowl with clean beaters until foamy. Gradually add remaining 2 tablespoons granulated sugar; beat until stiff but not dry peaks form.

4. Gently stir one fourth of egg whites into batter; fold in remaining whites. Spoon batter evenly into ungreased 10-inch tube pan.

5. Bake 45 to 50 minutes or until cake springs back when touched. Cool upside down 45 minutes before removing from pan. Sprinkle with powdered sugar just before serving, if desired.   *Makes 10 servings*

Tip: Invert the cake pan onto a narrow-necked bottle or a funnel to cool.

Lemon Chiffon Cake

Classic Boston Cream Pie

1 cup sugar
2 eggs
⅓ cup shortening
1 teaspoon vanilla extract
1¼ cups all-purpose flour
1½ teaspoons baking powder
¼ teaspoon salt
¾ cup milk
    Rich Filling (recipe follows)
    Dark Cocoa Glaze (page 12)

1. Heat oven to 350°F. Grease and flour 9-inch round baking pan.

2. Beat sugar, eggs, shortening and vanilla in large bowl until fluffy. Stir together flour, baking powder and salt; add alternately with milk to shortening mixture, beating well after each addition. Pour batter into prepared pan.

3. Bake 30 to 35 minutes or until wooden pick inserted in center comes out clean. Cool 10 minutes; remove from pan to wire rack. Cool completely.

4. Prepare Rich Filling. With long serrated knife, cut cake in half horizontally. Place one layer, cut side up, on serving plate; spread with prepared filling. Top with remaining layer, cut side down. Prepare Dark Cocoa Glaze; spread over cake, allowing glaze to run down sides. Refrigerate several hours or until cold. Garnish as desired. Refrigerate leftover pie.

Makes 8 to 10 servings

Rich Filling

⅓ cup sugar
2 tablespoons cornstarch
1½ cups milk
2 egg yolks, slightly beaten
1 tablespoon butter or margarine
1 teaspoon vanilla extract

continued on page 12

Classic Boston Cream Pie

Classic Boston Cream Pie, continued

Stir together sugar and cornstarch in medium saucepan; gradually add milk and egg yolks, stirring until blended. Cook over medium heat, stirring constantly, until mixture comes to a boil. Boil 1 minute, stirring constantly. Remove from heat; stir in butter and vanilla. Cover; refrigerate several hours or until cold. *Makes about 1⅓ cups filling*

Dark Cocoa Glaze

3 tablespoons water
2 tablespoons butter or margarine
3 tablespoons HERSHEY'S Cocoa
1 cup powdered sugar
½ teaspoon vanilla extract

Heat water and butter in small saucepan over medium heat until mixture comes to a boil; remove from heat. Immediately stir in cocoa. Gradually add powdered sugar and vanilla, beating with whisk until smooth and of desired consistency; cool slightly. *Makes about ¾ cup glaze*

Mom's Favorite White Cake

2¼ cups cake flour
1 tablespoon baking powder
½ teaspoon salt
1½ cups sugar
½ cup (1 stick) butter, softened
4 egg whites
2 teaspoons vanilla
1 cup milk
Strawberry Frosting (page 13)
Fruit Filling (page 13)
Fresh strawberries (optional)

1. Preheat oven to 350°F. Line bottoms of two 9-inch round cake pans with waxed paper; lightly grease paper. Combine flour, baking powder and salt in medium bowl.

2. Beat sugar and butter in large bowl with electric mixer at medium speed until light and fluffy. Add egg whites, 2 at a time, beating well after each addition. Add vanilla; beat until blended. Add flour mixture alternately with milk, beating well at low speed after each addition. Pour batter evenly into prepared pans.

3. Bake 25 minutes or until toothpick inserted into centers comes out clean. Cool cake layers in pans 10 minutes. Loosen edges with knife; remove to wire racks to cool completely.

4. Prepare Strawberry Frosting and Fruit Filling. Place one cake layer on serving plate; spread with Fruit Filling. Place second layer over filling; frost top and side of cake with Strawberry Frosting. Place strawberries on top of cake, if desired.

Makes 12 servings

Strawberry Frosting

2 envelopes (1.3 ounces each) whipped topping mix
⅔ cup milk
1 cup (6 ounces) white chocolate chips, melted
¼ cup strawberry jam

Beat whipped topping mix and milk in medium bowl with electric mixer at low speed until blended. Beat at high speed 4 minutes until topping thickens and peaks form. Beat melted chocolate into topping at low speed. Add jam; beat until blended. Chill 15 minutes or until spreading consistency.

Fruit Filling

1 cup Strawberry Frosting (recipe above)
1 can (8 ounces) crushed pineapple, drained
1 cup sliced strawberries

Combine Strawberry Frosting, pineapple and strawberries in medium bowl; mix well.

Pineapple Upside-Down Cake

Topping
- ½ cup (1 stick) butter or margarine
- 1 cup firmly packed brown sugar
- 1 can (20 ounces) pineapple slices, well drained
- Maraschino cherries, drained and halved
- Walnut halves

Cake
- 1 package DUNCAN HINES® Moist Deluxe® Pineapple Supreme Cake Mix
- 1 package (4-serving size) vanilla-flavor instant pudding and pie filling mix
- 4 eggs
- 1 cup water
- ½ cup oil

1. Preheat oven to 350°F.

2. For topping, melt butter over low heat in 12-inch cast-iron skillet or skillet with ovenproof handle. Remove from heat. Stir in brown sugar. Spread to cover bottom of skillet. Arrange pineapple slices, maraschino cherries and walnut halves in skillet. Set aside.

3. For cake, combine cake mix, pudding mix, eggs, water and oil in large mixing bowl. Beat at medium speed with electric mixer for 2 minutes. Pour batter evenly over fruit in skillet. Bake at 350°F for 1 hour or until toothpick inserted into center comes out clean. Invert onto serving plate.

Makes 16 to 20 servings

Tip: Cake can be made in a 13×9×2-inch pan. Bake at 350°F for 45 to 55 minutes or until toothpick inserted into center comes out clean. Cake is also delicious using Duncan Hines® Moist Deluxe® Classic Yellow Cake Mix.

Pineapple Upside-Down Cake

Orange Kiss Me Cakes

1 large orange
1 cup raisins
⅔ cup chopped walnuts, divided
2 cups all-purpose flour
1⅓ cups sugar, divided
1 teaspoon baking soda
1 teaspoon salt
1 cup milk, divided
½ cup shortening
2 eggs
1 teaspoon ground cinnamon

1. Preheat oven to 350°F. Lightly grease and flour six 1-cup mini bundt pans or one 12-cup bundt pan.

2. Juice orange; reserve ⅓ cup juice. Coarsely chop remaining orange pulp and peel. Process pulp, peel, raisins and ⅓ cup walnuts in food processor until finely ground.

3. Sift flour, 1 cup sugar, baking soda and salt into large bowl. Add ¾ cup milk and shortening; beat with electric mixer at medium speed 2 minutes or until well blended. Beat 2 minutes more. Add eggs and remaining ¼ cup milk; beat 2 minutes. Fold orange mixture into batter; mix well. Pour into prepared pans.

4. Bake 40 to 45 minutes or until toothpick inserted near centers comes out clean. Cool cakes in pans 15 minutes. Invert onto serving plate. Poke holes in cakes with wooden skewer or tines of fork.

5. Pour reserved orange juice over warm cakes. Combine remaining ⅓ cup sugar, ⅓ cup walnuts and cinnamon in small bowl. Sprinkle over cakes.   *Makes 6 cakes*

Grandma's® Gingerbread

½ cup shortening or butter
½ cup sugar
1 cup GRANDMA'S® Molasses
2 eggs
2½ cups all-purpose flour
2 teaspoons baking powder
2 teaspoons cinnamon
1 teaspoon salt
1 teaspoon ground ginger
½ teaspoon baking soda
½ teaspoon ground cloves
1 cup hot water

Heat oven to 350°F. In medium bowl, blend shortening with sugar. Add molasses and eggs; beat well. Sift dry ingredients; add alternately with water to molasses mixture. Bake in greased 9-inch square pan about 50 minutes.   *Makes 8 servings*

Hint: Just before serving, dust top of cake lightly with powdered sugar, if desired.

Editor's Note

We love this gingerbread recipe! It combines all the best features of this traditional cake—the rich, robust flavor of molasses and irresistible aroma of warm spices. Best of all, it's so quick and easy to make that you don't need to save it just for the holidays.

Grandma's® Gingerbread

Zesty Lemon Pound Cake

1 cup (6 ounces) NESTLÉ® TOLL HOUSE® Premier White Morsels
  or 3 bars (6-ounce box) NESTLÉ® TOLL HOUSE® Premier
  White Baking Bars, broken into pieces
2½ cups all-purpose flour
1 teaspoon baking powder
½ teaspoon salt
1 cup (2 sticks) butter, softened
1½ cups granulated sugar
2 teaspoons vanilla extract
3 large eggs
3 to 4 tablespoons freshly grated lemon peel (about 3 medium
  lemons)
1⅓ cups buttermilk
1 cup powdered sugar
3 tablespoons fresh lemon juice

PREHEAT oven to 350°F. Grease and flour 12-cup bundt pan.

MELT morsels in medium, uncovered, microwave-safe bowl on MEDIUM–HIGH (70%) power for 1 minute. STIR. Morsels may retain some of their original shape. If necessary, microwave at additional 10- to 15-second intervals, stirring just until morsels are melted. Cool slightly.

COMBINE flour, baking powder and salt in small bowl. Beat butter, granulated sugar and vanilla extract in large mixer bowl until creamy. Beat in eggs, one at a time, beating well after each addition. Beat in lemon peel and melted morsels. Gradually beat in flour mixture alternately with buttermilk. Pour into prepared bundt pan.

BAKE for 50 to 55 minutes or until wooden pick inserted into cake comes out clean. Cool in pan on wire rack for 10 minutes. Combine powdered sugar and lemon juice in small bowl. Make holes in cake with wooden pick; pour *half* of lemon glaze over cake. Let stand for 5 minutes. Invert onto plate. Make holes in top of cake; pour *remaining* glaze over cake. Cool completely before serving.   *Makes 16 servings*

Zesty Lemon Pound Cake

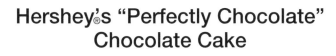

Hershey®'s "Perfectly Chocolate" Chocolate Cake

2 cups sugar
1¾ cups all-purpose flour
¾ cup HERSHEY'S Cocoa
1½ teaspoons baking powder
1½ teaspoons baking soda
1 teaspoon salt
1 cup milk
2 eggs
½ cup vegetable oil
2 teaspoons vanilla extract
1 cup boiling water
"Perfectly Chocolate" Chocolate Frosting (recipe follows)

1. Heat oven to 350°F. Grease and flour two 9-inch round baking pans.

2. Stir together sugar, flour, cocoa, baking powder, baking soda and salt in large bowl. Add milk, eggs, oil and vanilla; beat on medium speed of mixer 2 minutes. Stir in boiling water (batter will be thin). Pour batter evenly into prepared pans.

3. Bake 30 to 35 minutes or until wooden pick inserted into centers comes out clean. Cool 10 minutes; remove from pans to wire racks. Cool completely. Frost with "Perfectly Chocolate" Chocolate Frosting.

Makes 10 to 12 servings

"Perfectly Chocolate" Chocolate Frosting

½ cup (1 stick) butter or margarine
⅔ cup HERSHEY'S Cocoa
3 cups powdered sugar
⅓ cup milk
1 teaspoon vanilla extract

Melt butter. Stir in cocoa. Alternately add powdered sugar and milk, beating to spreading consistency. Add small amount additional milk, if needed. Stir in vanilla.

Makes about 2 cups frosting

Hershey's "Perfectly Chocolate" Chocolate Cake

Chocolate Sensations

Classic Chocolate Cake

2 cups all-purpose flour
⅔ cup unsweetened cocoa powder
1¼ teaspoons baking soda
1 teaspoon salt
¼ teaspoon baking powder
1 cup granulated sugar
¾ cup (1½ sticks) butter, softened
⅔ cup packed brown sugar
3 eggs
1 teaspoon vanilla
1⅓ cups water
Prepared chocolate frosting (optional)

1. Preheat oven to 350°F. Grease 13×9-inch baking pan.

2. Combine flour, cocoa, baking soda, salt and baking powder in medium bowl. Beat granulated sugar, butter and brown sugar in large bowl with electric mixer at medium-high speed 2 minutes or until light and creamy. Add eggs and vanilla; beat 2 minutes. Add flour mixture alternately with water; beat just until blended. Pour batter into prepared pan.

3. Bake 25 to 35 minutes or until toothpick inserted into center comes out clean. Cool cake in pan on wire rack. Frost with chocolate frosting, if desired. *Makes about 16 servings*

Orange-Glazed Cocoa Bundt Cake

1⅔ cups sugar
¾ cup (1½ sticks) butter or margarine, softened
2 eggs
1 teaspoon vanilla extract
¾ cup dairy sour cream
2 cups all-purpose flour
⅔ cup HERSHEY'S Cocoa
½ teaspoon salt
2 teaspoons baking soda
1 cup buttermilk or sour milk*
Orange Glaze or Vanilla Glaze (recipes follow)

To sour milk: Use 1 tablespoon white vinegar plus milk to equal 1 cup.

1. Heat oven to 350°F. Grease and flour 12-cup fluted tube pan.

2. Beat sugar, butter, eggs and vanilla in large bowl until light and fluffy; stir in sour cream. Stir together flour, cocoa and salt. Stir baking soda into buttermilk in medium bowl; add alternately with dry ingredients to butter mixture. Beat 2 minutes on medium speed. Pour batter into prepared pan.

3. Bake 50 minutes or until wooden pick inserted into center comes out clean. Cool in pan 10 minutes. Remove from pan to wire rack. Cool completely. Glaze with Orange Glaze; garnish as desired.

Makes 12 to 14 servings

Orange Glaze: Combine 2 cups powdered sugar, ¼ cup (½ stick) melted butter or margarine, 3 tablespoons orange juice, 1 teaspoon vanilla extract and ½ teaspoon freshly grated orange peel in medium bowl; beat until smooth. Makes 1 cup glaze.

Vanilla Glaze: Substitute 3 tablespoons water for orange juice and omit orange peel.

Orange-Glazed Cocoa Bundt Cake

Chocolate Strawberry Cream Cake

2 cups all-purpose flour
2 cups plus 3 tablespoons sugar, divided
½ cup unsweetened cocoa powder
2 teaspoons baking soda
½ teaspoon salt
1 cup warm water
½ cup vegetable oil
½ cup (1 stick) butter, melted
2 eggs, at room temperature
½ cup buttermilk
3 teaspoons vanilla, divided
1½ cups plus 3 tablespoons whipping cream, divided
1 cup (6 ounces) semisweet chocolate chips
½ cup strawberry jam
3 tablespoons sour cream
Fresh strawberries (optional)

1. Preheat oven to 350°F. Spray two 9-inch round cake pans with nonstick cooking spray. Line bottoms of pans with waxed paper or parchment paper; spray with cooking spray.

2. Whisk flour, 2 cups sugar, cocoa, baking soda and salt in large bowl until well blended. Whisk water, oil, butter, eggs, buttermilk and 2 teaspoons vanilla in medium bowl until well blended. Pour butter mixture into flour mixture; whisk or beat with electric mixer at low speed 2 minutes. Pour batter into prepared pans.

3. Bake 35 to 40 minutes or until toothpick inserted into centers comes out clean. Cool cake layers in pans 15 minutes; remove to wire racks to cool completely.

4. Meanwhile, place 3 tablespoons cream and chocolate chips in small microwavable bowl; microwave on HIGH 40 seconds. Stir until chocolate is melted and mixture is smooth. Set aside to cool to spreading consistency.

5. Place one cake layer on serving plate; spread with ¼ cup jam. Spread cooled chocolate mixture over jam. Top with second cake layer;

continued on page 30

Chocolate Strawberry Cream Cake

Chocolate Strawberry Cream Cake, continued

spread with ¼ cup jam. Cover loosely with plastic wrap and refrigerate 2 hours or up to 2 days.

6. Beat remaining 1½ cups cream, 3 tablespoons sugar, 1 teaspoon vanilla and sour cream in large bowl with electric mixer at medium-high speed just until stiff peaks form. *Do not overbeat.* Spread top and side of cake with whipped cream frosting. Refrigerate cake until ready to serve, up to 8 hours. Garnish with strawberries.   *Makes 14 servings*

Chocolate-Peanut Butter Oatmeal Snacking Cake

1¼ cups boiling water
1 cup uncooked old-fashioned oats
1 cup granulated sugar
1 cup packed brown sugar
½ cup (1 stick) butter, softened
2 eggs, beaten
1 teaspoon vanilla
1¾ cups all-purpose flour
¼ cup unsweetened cocoa powder
1 teaspoon baking soda
1 cup (6 ounces) semisweet chocolate chips
1 package (12 ounces) chocolate and peanut butter chips

1. Preheat oven to 350°F. Grease 13×9-inch baking pan.

2. Combine boiling water and oats in large bowl; let stand 10 minutes. Stir until water is absorbed. Add granulated sugar, brown sugar and butter; beat with electric mixer at low speed 1 minute or until well blended. Beat in eggs and vanilla until well blended.

3. Combine flour, cocoa and baking soda in medium bowl. Gradually beat into oat mixture until well blended; stir in 1 cup chocolate chips. Pour batter into prepared pan. Sprinkle with chocolate and peanut butter chips.

4. Bake 40 minutes or until toothpick inserted into center comes out clean. Cool completely in pan on wire rack.   *Makes about 16 servings*

Chocolate-Peanut Butter Oatmeal Snacking Cake

Rich Chocolate Torte

1 cup (2 sticks) plus 2 tablespoons unsalted butter, softened, divided
8 ounces bittersweet chocolate, chopped
4 eggs
1¼ cups sugar
⅓ cup cornstarch
1 tablespoon water
1 tablespoon vanilla
Unsweetened cocoa powder (optional)

1. Preheat oven to 350°F. Melt 2 tablespoons butter; brush on bottom and side of 9-inch springform pan. Wrap outside of pan with foil.

2. Place chocolate in small microwavable bowl. Microwave on HIGH 30 seconds; stir. Microwave at additional 15-second intervals until chocolate is melted and smooth; set aside to cool slightly.

3. Beat remaining 1 cup butter in medium bowl with electric mixer until light and fluffy. Add cooled chocolate; beat 2 minutes. Beat eggs in large bowl with electric mixer; slowly add sugar. Beat at high speed about 5 minutes or until mixture thickens and is pale in color. Sift cornstarch over mixture; stir to blend. Add chocolate mixture, water and vanilla; beat just until well blended. Pour batter into prepared pan.

4. Place springform pan in large roasting pan. Place pan in oven; carefully pour hot water into roasting pan to reach halfway up side of springform pan.

5. Bake 40 minutes or until center is just set. Remove springform pan from roasting pan; cool completely on wire rack. Remove side of pan; invert cake onto serving plate. Remove bottom of pan by sliding thin knife or spatula underneath to release. (Torte may be wrapped and refrigerated up to 3 days before serving.) Sift cocoa over top of torte.

Makes 12 servings

Variation: For a coffee-flavored torte, dissolve 1 tablespoon instant coffee or espresso powder in 2 tablespoons water. Add to batter with chocolate mixture instead of 1 tablespoon water and vanilla.

Rich Chocolate Torte

European Mocha Fudge Cake

1¼ cups (2½ sticks) butter or margarine
¾ cup HERSHEY'S SPECIAL DARK® Cocoa
4 eggs
1 teaspoon vanilla extract
¼ teaspoon salt
2 cups sugar
1 cup all-purpose flour
1 cup finely chopped pecans
Creamy Coffee Filling (recipe follows)
Chocolate curls (optional)

1. Heat oven to 350°F. Butter bottom and sides of two 9-inch round baking pans. Line bottoms with wax paper; butter paper.

2. Melt butter in small saucepan; remove from heat. Add cocoa, stirring until blended; cool slightly. Beat eggs in large bowl until foamy; add vanilla and salt. Gradually beat in sugar. Add cooled chocolate mixture; blend thoroughly. Fold in flour. Stir in pecans. Pour mixture into prepared pans.

3. Bake 20 to 25 minutes or until wooden pick inserted in centers comes out clean. Do not overbake. Cool 5 minutes; remove from pans to wire racks. Carefully peel off paper. Cool completely. Spread Creamy Coffee Filling between layers, over top and sides of cake. Garnish with chocolate curls, if desired. Refrigerate 1 hour or longer before serving.

Makes 10 to 12 servings

Make-Ahead Directions:
Cooled cake may be wrapped and frozen up to 4 weeks; thaw, wrapped, before filling and frosting.

Creamy Coffee Filling

1½ cups cold whipping cream
⅓ cup packed light brown sugar
2 teaspoons powdered instant coffee

Combine all ingredients; stir until instant coffee is almost dissolved. Beat until stiff.

Makes about 3 cups filling

European Mocha Fudge Cake

Chocolate Mint Fluff Roll

4 eggs, separated
¾ cup granulated sugar, divided
½ cup (1 stick) butter, softened
¼ cup crème de menthe liqueur
2 tablespoons water
1 teaspoon vanilla
⅔ cup cake flour
½ cup unsweetened cocoa powder
1 teaspoon baking powder
½ teaspoon salt
  Powdered sugar
  Chocolate Mint Filling (page 38)

1. Preheat oven to 375°F. Grease 15×10-inch jelly-roll pan. Line with parchment paper and grease again; dust with flour.

2. Beat egg whites in large bowl with electric mixer at high speed until soft peaks form. Gradually add ½ cup granulated sugar, beating until egg whites are stiff and glossy.

3. Beat egg yolks, remaining ¼ cup granulated sugar, butter, crème de menthe, water and vanilla in medium bowl with electric mixer about 4 minutes or until thick. Fold yolk mixture into egg white mixture.

4. Sift flour, cocoa, baking powder and salt into small bowl; fold flour mixture into egg mixture until blended. Pour batter into prepared pan.

5. Bake 12 to 15 minutes or until edges begin to pull away from sides of pan and center springs back when lightly touched. Dust clean kitchen towel with powdered sugar. Invert cake onto towel; peel off parchment paper. Starting from long side, gently roll up cake with towel. Cool cake completely. Prepare Chocolate Mint Filling.

6. Unroll cake; spread with filling. Roll up cake and place on serving plate. Sprinkle with additional powdered sugar. Chill before serving.

Makes 8 to 10 servings

continued on page 38

Chocolate Mint Fluff Roll

Chocolate Mint Fluff Roll, continued

Chocolate Mint Filling

1½ cups whipping cream
½ cup sugar
¼ cup unsweetened cocoa powder
¼ cup crème de menthe liqueur
½ teaspoon vanilla
    Pinch salt
1½ cups chopped chocolate mints

Beat cream, sugar, cocoa, crème de menthe, vanilla and salt in medium bowl with electric mixer at high speed until stiff peaks form. Gently fold in mints.

Sweetheart Chocolate Mini Bundt Cakes

1⅔ cups all-purpose flour
½ cup unsweetened cocoa powder
1 teaspoon baking soda
¼ teaspoon salt
1 cup plus 2 tablespoons buttermilk
¾ cup mayonnaise
¾ cup packed brown sugar
1 teaspoon vanilla
1 cup (6 ounces) semisweet chocolate chips, divided
¼ cup whipping cream

1. Preheat oven to 350°F. Spray 6 mini bundt pans with nonstick cooking spray.

2. Combine flour, cocoa, baking soda and salt in medium bowl. Beat buttermilk, mayonnaise, brown sugar and vanilla in large bowl with electric mixer at medium speed until well blended. Gradually add flour mixture; beat 2 minutes or until well blended. Stir in ½ cup chocolate chips. Spoon batter evenly into prepared pans.

3. Bake 22 minutes or until toothpick inserted near centers comes out clean. Cool cakes in pans 15 minutes; invert onto wire rack to cool completely.

4. Place remaining ½ cup chocolate chips in small bowl. Heat cream in small saucepan over low heat until bubbles form around edge of pan; pour over chips. Let stand 5 minutes; stir until smooth. Cool until slightly thickened; drizzle over cakes.   *Makes 6 cakes*

Molten Chocolate Cakes

2 tablespoons plus ¾ cup (1½ sticks) butter, divided
8 ounces NESTLÉ CHOCOLATIER™ 62% Cacao Bittersweet Chocolate Baking Bars, broken into pieces
3 large eggs
3 large egg yolks
¼ cup plus 1 tablespoon granulated sugar
1 teaspoon vanilla extract
1 tablespoon all-purpose flour
Powdered sugar

Preheat oven to 425°F. Generously butter six (6-ounce) ramekins or custard cups with 2 tablespoons butter.

Stir ¾ cup butter and chocolate in medium, heavy-duty saucepan over low heat until chocolate is melted and mixture is smooth. Remove from heat. Beat eggs, egg yolks, sugar and vanilla extract in large mixer bowl until thick and pale yellow, about 8 minutes. Fold one third of chocolate mixture into egg mixture. Fold in remaining chocolate mixture and flour until well blended. Divide batter evenly among prepared ramekins. Place on baking sheet.

Bake for 12 to 13 minutes or until sides are set and 1-inch centers move slightly when shaken. Remove from oven to wire rack.

Run a thin knife around top edge of cakes to loosen slightly; carefully invert onto serving plates. Lift ramekins off of cakes. Sprinkle with powdered sugar. Serve immediately.   *Makes 6 servings*

Chocolate Yogurt Snack Cake

⅔ cup plus 2 tablespoons unsweetened Dutch process
    cocoa powder, divided
1¾ cups all-purpose flour
  2 teaspoons baking powder
  1 teaspoon salt
½ teaspoon baking soda
  2 cups (16 ounces) whole-milk plain yogurt, divided
⅓ cup water
  1 teaspoon vanilla
1¼ cups granulated sugar
  6 tablespoons (¾ stick) butter, softened
  2 eggs
  1 package (12 ounces) semisweet chocolate chips
  1 cup powdered sugar, sifted

1. Preheat oven to 350°F. Spray 13×9-inch baking pan with nonstick
cooking spray. Dust with 2 tablespoons cocoa powder; tap out excess.

2. Combine remaining ⅔ cup cocoa, flour, baking powder, salt and baking
soda in medium bowl. Whisk 1 cup yogurt, water and vanilla in small bowl
until well blended.

3. Beat granulated sugar and butter in large bowl with electric mixer
at medium speed about 1 minute or until light and fluffy. Add eggs;
beat 1 minute. Gradually add flour mixture at low speed; beat just until
combined. Add yogurt mixture; beat 1 minute, scraping side of bowl once.
Pour batter into prepared pan.

4. Bake 35 to 40 minutes or until toothpick inserted into center comes
out clean. Cool cake completely in pan on wire rack.

5. Meanwhile, place chocolate chips and remaining 1 cup yogurt in
medium microwavable bowl. Microwave on HIGH 30 seconds; stir.
Microwave 10 seconds; stir. Continue microwaving at 10-second intervals
until chocolate is melted and mixture is smooth. Whisk in powdered sugar
until well blended. Cover and refrigerate about 1 hour, stirring occasionally,
or until frosting reaches spreading consistency. (Frosting will be soft.)
Spread over cooled cake. *Makes 12 servings*

Chocolate Yogurt Snack Cake

Triple Chocolate Cake

1½ cups sugar
¾ cup (1½ sticks) butter, softened
1 egg
1 teaspoon vanilla
2 cups all-purpose flour
⅔ cup unsweetened cocoa powder
2 teaspoons baking soda
¼ teaspoon salt
1 cup buttermilk
¾ cup sour cream
　Chocolate Ganache Filling (recipe follows)
　Easy Chocolate Frosting (recipe follows)

1. Preheat oven to 350°F. Grease and flour two 9-inch round cake pans. Beat sugar and butter in large bowl with electric mixer at medium speed until light and fluffy. Beat in egg and vanilla until blended. Combine flour, cocoa, baking soda and salt in medium bowl. Add to butter mixture alternately with buttermilk and sour cream, beginning and ending with flour mixture. Beat well after each addition. Pour batter into prepared pans.

2. Bake 30 to 35 minutes or until toothpick inserted into centers comes out clean. Cool cake layers in pans 10 minutes; remove to wire racks to cool completely. Cut each cake layer in half horizontally.

3. Meanwhile, prepare filling and frosting. Place one cake layer on serving plate. Spread with one third of filling. Repeat layers twice. Top with remaining cake layer. Frost top and side of cake.　　　　*Makes 12 to 16 servings*

Chocolate Ganache Filling: Bring ¾ cup whipping cream, 1 tablespoon butter and 1 tablespoon granulated sugar to a boil; stir until sugar is dissolved. Place 1½ cups semisweet chocolate chips in medium bowl; pour cream mixture over chocolate and let stand 5 minutes. Stir until smooth; let stand 15 minutes or until filling reaches desired consistency.

Easy Chocolate Frosting: Beat ½ cup (1 stick) softened butter in large bowl with electric mixer at medium speed until creamy. Add 4 cups powdered sugar and ¾ cup cocoa in batches alternately with ½ cup milk; beat until smooth. Stir in 1½ teaspoons vanilla.

Triple Chocolate Cake

Chocolate Lemon Marble Cake

2½ cups all-purpose flour
1¾ cups plus ⅓ cup sugar, divided
 2 teaspoons baking powder
1¼ teaspoons baking soda, divided
 ½ teaspoon salt
 ⅓ cup butter or margarine, softened
 ⅓ cup shortening
 3 eggs
1⅔ cups buttermilk or sour milk*
 2 teaspoons vanilla extract
 ⅓ cup HERSHEY'S Cocoa
 ¼ cup water
 2 teaspoons freshly grated lemon peel
 ¼ teaspoon lemon juice
   Cocoa Glaze (page 46)

To sour milk: Use 1 tablespoon plus 2 teaspoons white vinegar plus milk to equal 1⅔ cups.

1. Heat oven to 375°F. Grease and flour 12-cup fluted tube pan.**

2. Stir together flour, 1¾ cups sugar, baking powder, 1 teaspoon baking soda and salt in large bowl. Add butter, shortening, eggs, buttermilk and vanilla; beat on medium speed of electric mixer 3 minutes.

3. Stir together cocoa, remaining ⅓ cup sugar, remaining ¼ teaspoon baking soda and water; blend into ⅔ cup vanilla batter. Blend lemon peel and lemon juice into remaining vanilla batter; drop spoonfuls of lemon batter into prepared pan. Drop spoonfuls of chocolate batter on top of lemon batter; swirl with knife or metal spatula for marbled effect.

4. Bake 35 to 40 minutes or until wooden pick inserted in center comes out clean. Cool 15 minutes; remove from pan to wire rack. Cool completely. Glaze with Cocoa Glaze.   *Makes 16 to 18 servings*

**Cake may also be baked in 2 (9×5×3-inch) loaf pans. Bake 40 to 45 minutes or until wooden pick inserted in center comes out clean.*

continued on page 46

Chocolate Lemon Marble Cake

Chocolate Lemon Marble Cake, continued

Cocoa Glaze

¼ cup **HERSHEY'S Cocoa**
3 tablespoons light corn syrup
4 teaspoons water
½ teaspoon vanilla extract
1 cup powdered sugar

Heat cocoa, corn syrup and water in small saucepan over medium heat, stirring constantly, until mixture thickens. Remove from heat; blend in vanilla and powdered sugar until smooth.   *Makes about 1½ cups*

German Chocolate Cake

1 (18.25- or 18.5-ounce) package German chocolate cake mix
1 cup water
3 eggs, plus 1 egg yolk
½ cup vegetable oil
1 (14-ounce) can **EAGLE BRAND®** Sweetened Condensed Milk
  (NOT evaporated milk), divided
3 tablespoons butter or margarine
1 egg yolk
⅓ cup chopped pecans
⅓ cup flaked coconut
1 teaspoon vanilla extract

1. Preheat oven to 350°F. In large bowl, combine cake mix, water, 3 eggs, oil and ⅓ cup EAGLE BRAND®. Beat on low speed until moistened, then beat on high speed 2 minutes. Pour into well-greased and floured 13×9-inch baking pan.

2. Bake 40 to 45 minutes or until toothpick inserted near center comes out clean.

3. In small saucepan over low heat, combine remaining EAGLE BRAND®, butter and egg yolk. Cook and stir until thickened, about 6 minutes. Add pecans, coconut and vanilla; spread over warm cake. Store leftovers covered in refrigerator.   *Makes one (13×9-inch) cake*

German Chocolate Cake

Aunt Lucille's Chocolate Pound Cake

3 cups all-purpose flour
5 tablespoons unsweetened cocoa powder
1 tablespoon baking powder
¼ teaspoon salt
½ cup (1 stick) butter, softened
½ cup shortening
3 cups sugar
4 eggs
1 cup sweetened condensed milk
1 teaspoon vanilla
    Chocolate Glaze (recipe follows)

1. Preheat oven to 300°F. Grease 12-cup bundt pan.

2. Sift flour into medium bowl. Sift again with cocoa, baking powder and salt.

3. Beat butter and shortening in large bowl with electric mixer at medium speed 1 minute. Gradually beat in sugar. Add eggs, 1 at a time, beating well after each addition until blended. Add flour mixture, condensed milk and vanilla; mix well. Pour into prepared pan.

4. Bake 1 hour or until toothpick inserted near center comes out clean. Cool completely in pan on wire rack.

5. Meanwhile, prepare Chocolate Glaze. Invert cake onto serving plate. Pour glaze over cake. *Makes 12 servings*

Chocolate Glaze: Combine ¾ cup sweetened condensed milk and 2 ounces unsweetened chocolate, chopped, in medium saucepan. Cook and stir over low heat until slightly thickened. Add 2 cups sugar; bring to a boil. Boil 9 to 10 minutes, stirring constantly. Remove from heat. Add ¼ cup (½ stick) butter and ¼ teaspoon salt; stir until butter is melted. Stir in 1 teaspoon vanilla. Cool 20 minutes before using.

Aunt Lucille's Chocolate Pound Cake

Family Favorites

Apple Spice Custard Cake

1 (18.25-ounce) package spice cake mix
2 medium apples, peeled, cored and chopped
1 (14-ounce) can EAGLE BRAND® Sweetened Condensed Milk
   (NOT evaporated milk)
1 (8-ounce) container sour cream
¼ cup lemon juice
   Ground cinnamon (optional)

1. Preheat oven to 350°F. Grease and flour 13×9-inch baking pan.

2. Prepare cake mix according to package directions. Stir in apples. Pour batter into prepared pan. Bake 30 to 35 minutes or until toothpick inserted near center comes out clean.

3. In medium bowl, combine EAGLE BRAND® and sour cream; mix well. Stir in lemon juice. Remove cake from oven; spread sour cream mixture evenly over hot cake.

4. Return to oven; bake 5 minutes or until set. Sprinkle with cinnamon (optional). Cool. Chill. Store leftovers covered in refrigerator.

Makes one (13×9-inch) cake

Prep Time: 15 minutes • **Bake Time:** 35 to 40 minutes

Banana Cake

2½ cups all-purpose flour
1 tablespoon baking soda
½ teaspoon salt
1 cup granulated sugar
¾ cup packed light brown sugar
½ cup (1 stick) butter, softened
2 eggs
1 teaspoon vanilla
3 ripe bananas, mashed (about 1⅔ cups)
⅔ cup buttermilk
1 container (16 ounces) dark chocolate frosting

1. Preheat oven to 350°F. Grease two 8-inch round cake pans. Combine flour, baking soda and salt in medium bowl.

2. Beat granulated sugar, brown sugar and butter in large bowl with electric mixer at medium speed until well blended. Add eggs and vanilla; beat well. Stir in bananas. Add flour mixture and buttermilk alternately to banana mixture; beat until well blended. Pour batter into prepared pans.

3. Bake about 35 minutes or until toothpick inserted into centers comes out clean. Cool cake layers in pans 10 minutes; remove to wire racks to cool completely.

4. Fill and frost cake with chocolate frosting.

Makes 12 to 16 servings

Banana Cake

Brickle Bundt Cake

1⅓ cups (8-ounce package) HEATH® BITS 'O BRICKLE® Toffee Bits, divided
1¼ cups granulated sugar, divided
¼ cup chopped walnuts
1 teaspoon ground cinnamon
½ cup (1 stick) butter, softened
2 eggs
1¼ teaspoons vanilla extract, divided
2 cups all-purpose flour
1½ teaspoons baking powder
1 teaspoon baking soda
¼ teaspoon salt
1 container (8 ounces) dairy sour cream
¼ cup (½ stick) butter, melted
1 cup powdered sugar
1 to 3 tablespoons milk, divided

1. Heat oven to 325°F. Grease and flour 12-cup fluted tube pan or 10-inch tube pan. Set aside ¼ cup toffee bits for topping. Combine remaining toffee bits, ¼ cup granulated sugar, walnuts and cinnamon; set aside.

2. Beat remaining 1 cup granulated sugar and ½ cup butter in large bowl until fluffy. Add eggs and 1 teaspoon vanilla; beat well. Stir together flour, baking powder, baking soda and salt; gradually add to butter mixture alternately with sour cream, beating until blended. Beat 3 minutes. Spoon one third of batter into prepared pan. Sprinkle with half of toffee mixture. Spoon half of remaining batter into pan. Top with remaining toffee mixture. Spoon remaining batter into pan. Pour melted butter over batter.

3. Bake 45 to 50 minutes or until wooden pick inserted near center comes out clean. Cool 10 minutes; remove from pan to wire rack. Cool completely.

4. Stir together powdered sugar, 1 tablespoon milk and remaining ¼ teaspoon vanilla. Stir in additional milk, 1 teaspoon at a time, until desired consistency; drizzle over cake. Sprinkle with reserved ¼ cup toffee bits. *Makes 12 to 14 servings*

Brickle Bundt Cake

Easy Apple Butter Cake

1 package (about 18 ounces) yellow cake mix *without* pudding
    in the mix
1 package (4-serving size) vanilla instant pudding and
    pie filling mix
1 cup sour cream
1 cup apple butter
4 eggs
½ cup apple juice
¼ cup vegetable oil
1 teaspoon ground cinnamon
½ teaspoon ground nutmeg
½ teaspoon ground cloves
¼ teaspoon salt
    Powdered sugar (optional)

1. Preheat oven to 375°F. Spray 10-inch tube pan with nonstick cooking spray.

2. Beat cake mix, pudding mix, sour cream, apple butter, eggs, apple juice, oil, cinnamon, nutmeg, cloves and salt in large bowl with electric mixer at low speed 1 minute. Beat at medium speed 2 minutes or until well blended and fluffy. Pour batter into prepared pan.

3. Bake 45 to 50 minutes or until toothpick inserted near center comes out clean. Cool in pan on wire rack 20 minutes. Run sharp knife along edge of pan to release cake; invert cake onto serving plate. Cool completely.

4. For decoration, place 9-inch paper doily over cake just before serving. Sift powdered sugar over doily; carefully remove doily.

Makes 12 servings

Easy Apple Butter Cake

Blueberry Crumb Cake

Crumb Topping (recipe follows)
2 cups all-purpose flour
⅔ cup sugar
1 tablespoon baking powder
1 teaspoon salt
½ teaspoon baking soda
1 cup milk
½ cup (1 stick) butter, melted
2 eggs, beaten
2 tablespoons lemon juice
2 cups fresh or thawed frozen blueberries

1. Preheat oven to 375°F. Grease 13×9-inch baking pan.

2. Prepare Crumb Topping; set aside.

3. Sift flour, sugar, baking powder, salt and baking soda into large bowl. Combine milk, butter, eggs and lemon juice in medium bowl. Pour into flour mixture; stir until blended.

4. Pour batter into prepared pan. Sprinkle blueberries evenly over batter. Sprinkle cake with Crumb Topping.

5. Bake 40 to 45 minutes or until toothpick inserted into center comes out clean. Serve warm.   *Makes 12 to 16 servings*

Crumb Topping: Combine 1 cup chopped walnuts or pecans, ⅔ cup sugar, ½ cup all-purpose flour, ¼ cup (½ stick) softened butter and ½ teaspoon ground cinnamon in large bowl until mixture forms coarse crumbs.

Blueberry Crumb Cake

Cookies 'n' Cream Cake

1 package (about 18 ounces) white cake mix *without* pudding
    in the mix
1 package (4-serving size) white chocolate instant pudding
    and pie filling mix
1 cup vegetable oil
4 egg whites
½ cup milk
20 chocolate sandwich cookies, coarsely chopped
½ cup semisweet chocolate chips
1 teaspoon shortening
4 chocolate sandwich cookies, cut into quarters

1. Preheat oven to 350°F. Spray 12-cup bundt pan with nonstick cooking
spray.

2. Beat cake mix, pudding mix, oil, egg whites and milk in large bowl
with electric mixer at medium speed 2 minutes. Stir in chopped cookies;
pour batter into prepared pan.

3. Bake 50 to 60 minutes or until cake springs back when lightly touched.
Cool 1 hour in pan on wire rack. Invert cake onto serving plate; cool
completely.

4. Combine chocolate chips and shortening in small microwavable bowl.
Microwave on HIGH 1 minute; stir. Microwave at 15-second intervals, as
necessary, stirring until melted and smooth. Drizzle glaze over cake; top
with quartered cookies. *Makes 10 to 12 servings*

Cookies 'n' Cream Cake

Oat-Apricot Snack Cake

1 container (6 ounces) plain yogurt (not fat free)
¾ cup packed brown sugar
½ cup granulated sugar
⅓ cup vegetable oil
1 egg
2 tablespoons milk
2 teaspoons vanilla
1 cup all-purpose flour
½ cup whole wheat flour
1 teaspoon baking soda
1 teaspoon cinnamon
½ teaspoon salt
2 cups old-fashioned oats
1 cup (about 6 ounces) chopped dried apricots
1 cup powdered sugar
2 tablespoons milk

1. Preheat oven to 350°F. Spray 13×9-inch baking pan with nonstick cooking spray.

2. Stir yogurt, brown sugar, granulated sugar, oil, egg, milk and vanilla in large bowl until well blended. Sift all-purpose flour, whole wheat flour, baking soda, cinnamon and salt into medium bowl. Add flour mixture to yogurt mixture; mix well. Stir in oats and apricots until blended. Pour batter into prepared pan.

3. Bake 25 to 30 minutes or until toothpick inserted into center comes out clean. Cool completely in pan on wire rack.

4. Stir powdered sugar and milk in small bowl until smooth. Spoon glaze into small resealable food storage bag; seal bag. Cut small hole from one corner of bag; drizzle glaze over cake. *Makes 32 servings*

Oat-Apricot Snack Cake

Lemony Pound Cake

1 package (4-serving size) lemon-flavor gelatin
¾ cup boiling water
1 package DUNCAN HINES® Moist Deluxe® Classic Yellow
   Cake Mix
4 eggs
¾ cup vegetable oil
1 can (6 ounces) frozen lemonade concentrate, thawed
½ cup granulated sugar

1. Preheat oven to 350°F. Grease and flour 10-inch tube pan.

2. Dissolve gelatin in water in large mixing bowl; cool. Stir in cake mix, eggs and oil. Beat at medium speed with electric mixer for 2 minutes. Spoon into prepared pan. Bake 50 minutes or until toothpick inserted in center comes out clean. Mix lemonade concentrate and sugar in small bowl. Pour over hot cake; cool in pan 1 hour. Remove from pan. Cool completely. *Makes 12 to 16 servings*

Tip: Serve this cake with fresh or thawed frozen strawberries for a special dessert.

Editor's Note

It's so simple, but it's still sensational—when a standard cake mix gets a double dose of intense lemon flavor, the results are irresistible. A crowd-pleasing cake that can be whipped up in a snap (or made a day or two ahead) is a sure-fire winner in our book!

Lemony Pound Cake

Lazy-Daisy Cake

2 cups granulated sugar
4 eggs
½ cup (1 stick) butter, softened, divided
2 teaspoons vanilla
2 cups all-purpose flour
2 teaspoons baking powder
1 cup warm milk
1 cup flaked coconut
½ cup plus 2 tablespoons packed brown sugar
⅓ cup half-and-half

1. Preheat oven to 350°F. Grease 13×9-inch baking pan.

2. Beat granulated sugar, eggs, ¼ cup butter and vanilla in large bowl with electric mixer at medium speed 3 minutes until fluffy. Sift flour and baking powder into medium bowl. Beat into egg mixture until well blended. Stir in milk. Pour batter into prepared pan.

3. Bake 30 minutes or until toothpick inserted into center comes out clean.

4. Meanwhile, combine remaining 4 tablespoons butter, coconut, brown sugar and half-and-half in medium saucepan over medium heat. Cook until sugar dissolves and butter melts, stirring constantly.

5. Spread coconut mixture over warm cake. Broil 4 inches from heat source 2 to 3 minutes or until top is light golden brown.

Makes 12 to 14 servings

Lazy-Daisy Cake

Glazed Applesauce Spice Cake

¾ cup (1½ sticks) butter, softened
1 cup packed light brown sugar
3 eggs
1½ teaspoons vanilla
2¼ cups all-purpose flour
2 teaspoons baking soda
2 teaspoons ground cinnamon
¾ teaspoon ground nutmeg
½ teaspoon ground ginger
¼ teaspoon salt
1½ cups unsweetened applesauce
½ cup milk
⅔ cup chopped walnuts
⅔ cup butterscotch chips
Apple Glaze (recipe follows)

1. Preheat oven to 350°F. Grease and lightly flour 12-cup bundt pan or 10-inch tube pan.

2. Beat butter and brown sugar in large bowl until light and fluffy. Beat in eggs and vanilla until well blended. Combine flour, baking soda, cinnamon, nutmeg, ginger and salt in medium bowl. Add flour mixture to butter mixture alternately with applesauce and milk, beginning and ending with flour mixture, beating well after each addition. Stir in walnuts and butterscotch chips. Pour batter into prepared pan.

3. Bake 45 to 50 minutes or until toothpick inserted near center comes out clean. Cool cake in pan 15 minutes; invert onto wire rack to cool completely.

4. Prepare Apple Glaze and spoon over top of cake. Store tightly covered at room temperature. *Makes 12 servings*

Apple Glaze: Place 1 cup sifted powdered sugar in small bowl. Stir in 2 to 3 tablespoons apple juice concentrate to make stiff glaze.

Glazed Applesauce Spice Cake

Sweet and Sour Brunch Cake

1 package (16 ounces) frozen rhubarb, thawed and patted dry
1 cup packed brown sugar
1 tablespoon all-purpose flour
1 teaspoon ground cinnamon
¼ cup (½ stick) butter, diced
1 package (about 18 ounces) yellow cake mix *without* pudding in the mix
1 package (4-serving size) vanilla instant pudding and pie filling mix
½ cup water
½ cup vegetable oil
4 eggs
⅔ cup sour cream

1. Preheat oven to 350°F. Spray 13×9-inch baking pan with nonstick cooking spray.

2. Spread rhubarb evenly in single layer in prepared pan. Combine brown sugar, flour and cinnamon in small bowl; mix well. Sprinkle evenly over rhubarb; dot with butter.

3. Beat cake mix, pudding mix, water, oil, eggs and sour cream in large bowl with electric mixer at low speed 1 minute. Beat at medium speed 2 minutes or until well blended and creamy. Pour batter into prepared pan, spreading carefully over rhubarb mixture.

4. Bake 40 to 50 minutes or until toothpick inserted into center comes out clean. Cool cake in pan 5 minutes; invert onto serving platter.

Makes 16 to 18 servings

Note: If frozen rhubarb is unavailable, substitute frozen unsweetened strawberries.

Sweet and Sour Brunch Cake

Lemon Poppy Seed Bundt Cake

1 cup granulated sugar
½ cup (1 stick) butter, softened
1 egg, at room temperature
2 egg whites, at room temperature
¾ cup milk
2 teaspoons vanilla
2 cups all-purpose flour
2 tablespoons poppy seeds
1 tablespoon grated lemon peel
2 teaspoons baking powder
¼ teaspoon salt
Powdered sugar

1. Preheat oven to 350°F. Grease and flour 12-cup bundt pan.

2. Beat granulated sugar, butter, egg and egg whites in large bowl with electric mixer at medium speed until well blended. Add milk and vanilla; beat until blended. Add flour, poppy seeds, lemon peel, baking powder and salt; beat about 2 minutes or until smooth. Pour into prepared pan.

3. Bake 30 minutes or until toothpick inserted near center comes out clean. Cool cake in pan 10 minutes; gently loosen cake from pan with knife. Invert onto wire rack to cool completely. Sprinkle with powdered sugar just before serving.

Makes 16 servings

Kitchen Tip

With so many ridges, bundt pans can be difficult to grease—and if your pan is not well greased, then the cake might not come out. For the best coverage, use melted butter and a pastry brush to coat the pan evenly before dusting with flour. Or, use a nonstick baking spray that contains flour instead.

Lemon Poppy Seed Bundt Cake

Cranberry Pound Cake

1½ cups sugar
1 cup (2 sticks) unsalted butter
¼ teaspoon salt
¼ teaspoon ground mace or nutmeg
4 eggs
2 cups cake flour
1 cup chopped fresh or frozen cranberries

1. Preheat oven to 350°F. Grease and flour 9×5-inch loaf pan.

2. Beat sugar, butter, salt and mace in large bowl with electric mixer at medium speed until light and fluffy. Beat in eggs, 1 at a time, until well blended. Reduce speed to low; add flour, ½ cup at a time, scraping down side of bowl occasionally. Fold in cranberries. Spoon batter into prepared pan.

3. Bake 60 to 70 minutes or until toothpick inserted into center comes out clean. Cool cake in pan on wire rack 5 minutes. Run knife around edges of pan to loosen cake; cool additional 30 minutes in pan. Remove to wire rack to cool completely.   *Makes 12 servings*

Note: You can make this cake when fresh or frozen cranberries aren't available. Cover 1 cup dried sweetened cranberries with hot water; let stand 10 minutes. Drain well before using.

Cranberry Pound Cake

Fancy & Delicious

Black Forest Angel Food Cake

1 package (about 16 ounces) angel food cake mix
½ cup unsweetened cocoa powder
1½ cups water
1 can (12 ounces) cherry pie filling
2 tablespoons cherry liqueur (optional)
1 cup whipping cream
2 tablespoons powdered sugar

1. Preheat oven to 350°F.

2. Pour cake mix into large bowl; sift cocoa over cake mix. Add water; whisk 1 to 2 minutes or until well blended. Pour batter into ungreased 10-inch tube pan. Bake and cool according to package directions.

3. Place cherry pie filling in microwavable bowl; microwave on HIGH 1 minute or until heated through. Stir in liqueur, if desired.

4. Beat cream and sugar in medium bowl with electric mixer at medium-high speed until stiff peaks form. Cut cake horizontally into 3 layers. Place bottom layer on serving plate; top with half of whipped cream and cherries. Top with center layer, remaining whipped cream, remaining cherries and top layer of cake. *Makes 12 to 16 servings*

Ginger Spice Roll

3 eggs, separated
½ cup (1 stick) butter, softened
½ cup light molasses
¼ cup granulated sugar
1 cup all-purpose flour
¾ teaspoon baking soda
½ teaspoon ground ginger
½ teaspoon ground cinnamon
½ teaspoon ground cloves
¼ teaspoon ground nutmeg
　Powdered sugar
　Spiced Filling (recipe follows)

1. Preheat oven to 375°F. Grease 15×10×1-inch jelly-roll pan. Line pan with parchment paper and grease; dust pan with flour.

2. Beat egg yolks in large bowl with electric mixer at high speed 4 minutes or until thick and lemon colored. Add butter and molasses; beat 1 minute.

3. Beat egg whites in medium bowl until foamy. Add granulated sugar; beat until soft peaks form. Fold into egg yolk mixture. Sift flour, baking soda, ginger, cinnamon, cloves and nutmeg into small bowl. Fold into egg mixture until well blended. Pour batter into prepared pan.

4. Bake 10 to 12 minutes or until cake is golden and edges begin to pull away from sides of pan. Dust clean kitchen towel with powdered sugar. Invert cake onto towel; peel off parchment paper. Starting from short side, gently roll up cake with towel. Cool cake completely.

5. Prepare Spiced Filling. Unroll cake; spread with filling. Roll up cake; sprinkle with powdered sugar. 　　　　　　　*Makes 8 to 10 servings*

Spiced Filling: Beat 1 package (8 ounces) cream cheese and ¼ cup (½ stick) butter in medium bowl with electric mixer until well blended and fluffy. Stir in 1 cup powdered sugar, ½ teaspoon vanilla, ¼ teaspoon ground ginger and ¼ teaspoon ground cinnamon; mix well.

Ginger Spice Roll

Coconut Lemon Torte

1 (14-ounce) can EAGLE BRAND® Sweetened Condensed Milk
　(NOT evaporated milk)
2 egg yolks
½ cup lemon juice
1 teaspoon grated lemon rind (optional)
　Yellow food coloring (optional)
1 (18.25- or 18.5-ounce) package white cake mix
1 (4-ounce) container frozen nondairy whipped topping, thawed
　(about 1¾ cups)
　Flaked coconut

1. In medium saucepan, combine EAGLE BRAND®, egg yolks, lemon juice, lemon rind (optional) and food coloring (optional). Over medium heat, cook and stir until slightly thickened, about 10 minutes. Chill.

2. Preheat oven to 350°F. Prepare cake mix as package directs. Pour batter into two greased and floured 9-inch round cake pans.

3. Bake 30 minutes or until toothpick inserted near centers comes out clean. Remove from pans. Cool.

4. With sharp knife, remove crust from top of each cake. Split into layers. Spread equal portions of lemon mixture between layers and on top to within 1 inch of edge.

5. Frost side and 1-inch rim on top of cake with whipped topping. Coat side of cake with coconut; garnish as desired. Store leftovers covered in refrigerator.　　　　　　　　　　　　　*Makes one (9-inch) cake*

Prep Time: 15 minutes • **Bake Time:** 30 minutes

Coconut Lemon Torte

Pecan Praline Brandy Cake

1 package (about 18 ounces) butter pecan cake mix
¾ cup water
⅓ cup plain yogurt
2 egg whites
1 egg
¼ cup plus ½ teaspoon brandy, divided
2 tablespoons vegetable oil
1 cup chopped toasted pecans, divided
⅔ cup packed light brown sugar
⅓ cup light corn syrup
¼ cup whipping cream
2 tablespoons butter
½ teaspoon vanilla

1. Preheat oven to 350°F. Spray 10- or 12-cup bundt pan with nonstick cooking spray.

2. Beat cake mix, water, yogurt, egg whites, egg, ¼ cup brandy and oil in medium bowl with electric mixer at low speed 30 seconds. Beat at medium speed 2 minutes or until light and fluffy. Fold in ½ cup pecans. Pour batter into prepared pan.

3. Bake 50 to 60 minutes or until toothpick inserted near center comes out clean. Cool cake in pan 10 minutes; invert onto wire rack to cool completely.

4. Combine brown sugar, corn syrup, cream and butter in small saucepan. Bring to a boil over medium heat, stirring constantly. Remove from heat; stir in remaining ½ cup pecans, ½ teaspoon brandy and vanilla. Cool to room temperature (glaze should be thick but still pourable). Pour glaze over top of cake.   *Makes 12 servings*

Pecan Praline Brandy Cake

Chocolate Almond Torte

4 eggs, separated
¾ cup sugar, divided
¾ cup ground blanched almonds
⅓ cup all-purpose flour
⅓ cup HERSHEY'S Cocoa
½ teaspoon baking soda
¼ teaspoon salt
¼ cup water
1 teaspoon vanilla extract
¼ teaspoon almond extract
  Cherry Filling (page 86)
  Chocolate Glaze (page 86)
  Sliced almonds, maraschino cherries or candied cherries, halved

1. Heat oven to 375°F. Grease bottoms of three 8-inch round baking pans. Line bottoms with wax paper; grease paper.

2. Beat egg yolks on medium speed of electric mixer 3 minutes in medium bowl. Gradually add ½ cup sugar; continue beating 2 minutes. Stir together almonds, flour, cocoa, baking soda and salt; add alternately with water to egg yolk mixture, beating on low speed just until blended. Stir in vanilla and almond extract.

3. Beat egg whites in large bowl until foamy; gradually add remaining ¼ cup sugar, beating until stiff peaks form. Fold small amount beaten egg whites into chocolate mixture; gently fold chocolate mixture into remaining whites just until blended. Spread batter evenly in prepared pans.

4. Bake 16 to 18 minutes or until top springs back when touched lightly in center. Cool 10 minutes; remove from pans to wire racks. Cool completely.

5. Prepare Cherry Filling. Place one cake layer on serving plate; spread half of filling over top. Repeat, ending with plain layer on top. Prepare Chocolate Glaze; spread on top of cake, allowing glaze to run down sides. Garnish with almonds and cherry halves. Refrigerate until glaze is set. Cover; refrigerate leftover torte. *Makes 10 to 12 servings*

continued on page 86

Chocolate Almond Torte

Chocolate Almond Torte, continued

Cherry Filling

1 cup (½ pint) cold whipping cream
¼ cup powdered sugar
1½ teaspoons kirsch (cherry brandy) *or* ¼ teaspoon almond extract
⅓ cup chopped red candied cherries

Beat whipping cream, powdered sugar and kirsch until stiff; fold in
cherries.   *Makes about 2 cups filling*

Chocolate Glaze

1 tablespoon butter or margarine
2 tablespoons HERSHEY'S Cocoa
2 tablespoons water
1 cup powdered sugar
¼ teaspoon vanilla extract

Melt butter in small saucepan over low heat; add cocoa and water,
stirring constantly until slightly thickened. Remove from heat; gradually
add powdered sugar and vanilla, beating with whisk until smooth and
of spreading consistency. Add additional water, ½ teaspoon at a time,
if needed.   *Makes about ¾ cup glaze*

Editor's Note

This special-occasion torte is a spectacular
dessert—almost too beautiful to eat! Three
layers of tender chocolate cake are dressed
up with almond and cherry flavors to create
an irresistible cake that will impress any guest.

Fig and Hazelnut Cake

¾ cup hazelnuts (about 4 ounces) with skins removed,
  coarsely chopped
¾ cup whole dried figs (about 4 ounces), coarsely chopped
⅔ cup slivered blanched almonds (about 3 ounces), coarsely
  chopped
3 squares (1 ounce each) semisweet chocolate, finely chopped
⅓ cup diced candied orange peel
⅓ cup diced candied lemon peel
1¼ cups all-purpose flour
1¾ teaspoons baking powder
¾ teaspoon salt
3 eggs
½ cup sugar

1. Preheat oven to 300°F. Grease 8×4-inch loaf pan.

2. Combine hazelnuts, figs, almonds, chocolate and candied orange and lemon peels in medium bowl; mix well. Combine flour, baking powder and salt in small bowl.

3. Beat eggs and sugar in large bowl with electric mixer at high speed 5 minutes or until thick and pale yellow. Gently fold hazelnut mixture into egg mixture. Sift half of flour mixture over egg mixture; gently fold until blended. Repeat with remaining flour mixture. Spread batter evenly in prepared pan.

4. Bake 60 to 70 minutes or until top is golden brown and firm to the touch. Cool cake in pan 5 minutes; remove to wire rack to cool completely.   *Makes 12 servings*

Classic Chocolate-Buttermilk Birthday Cake

1 package (about 18 ounces) chocolate fudge cake mix
1 package (4-serving size) chocolate instant pudding and
    pie filling mix
1⅓ cups buttermilk
4 eggs
½ cup vegetable oil
2 tablespoons unsweetened cocoa powder
2 teaspoons vanilla, divided
1½ cups sugar
1 cup whipping cream
½ cup (1 stick) butter
6 ounces unsweetened chocolate, chopped

1. Preheat oven to 350°F. Spray two 9-inch round cake pans with nonstick cooking spray.

2. Beat cake mix, pudding mix, buttermilk, eggs, oil, cocoa and 1 teaspoon vanilla in large bowl with electric mixer at low speed 1 minute. Beat at medium speed 2 minutes or until well blended and fluffy. Pour batter into prepared pans.

3. Bake 25 to 30 minutes or until toothpick inserted into centers comes out clean. Cool cake layers in pans 10 minutes; remove to wire racks to cool completely.

4. Heat sugar and cream in small saucepan over medium-high heat, stirring until sugar is dissolved. When cream begins to bubble, reduce heat and simmer 5 minutes. Remove from heat; stir in butter and chocolate until melted and smooth. Stir in remaining 1 teaspoon vanilla. Pour into medium bowl; refrigerate until frosting is cool and thickened.

5. Place one cake layer on plate; spread with frosting. Top with second layer; frost top and side of cake with remaining frosting. Refrigerate at least 1 hour before serving. Refrigerate leftovers.   *Makes 16 servings*

Classic Chocolate-Buttermilk Birthday Cake

Pumpkin Carrot Cake

2 cups all-purpose flour
2 teaspoons baking soda
2 teaspoons ground cinnamon
½ teaspoon salt
¾ cup milk
1½ teaspoons lemon juice
3 large eggs
1¼ cups LIBBY'S® 100% Pure Pumpkin
1½ cups granulated sugar
½ cup packed brown sugar
½ cup vegetable oil
1 can (8 ounces) crushed pineapple, drained
1 cup (about 3 medium) grated carrots
1 cup flaked coconut
1¼ cups chopped nuts, *divided*
Cream Cheese Frosting (recipe follows)

PREHEAT oven to 350°F. Grease two 9-inch round baking pans.

COMBINE flour, baking soda, cinnamon and salt in small bowl. Combine milk and lemon juice in liquid measuring cup (mixture will appear curdled).

BEAT eggs, pumpkin, granulated sugar, brown sugar, oil, pineapple, carrots and milk mixture in large mixer bowl; mix well. Gradually add flour mixture; beat until combined. Stir in coconut and *1 cup* nuts. Pour into prepared baking pans.

BAKE for 30 to 35 minutes or until wooden pick inserted in center comes out clean. Cool in pans for 15 minutes. Remove to wire racks to cool completely.

FROST between layers, on side and top of cake with Cream Cheese Frosting. Garnish with *remaining* nuts. Store in refrigerator.

Makes 12 servings

Cream Cheese Frosting: **COMBINE** 11 ounces softened cream cheese, ⅓ cup softened butter and 3½ cups sifted powdered sugar in large mixer bowl until fluffy. Add 1 teaspoon vanilla extract, 2 teaspoons orange juice and 1 teaspoon grated orange peel; beat until combined.

Pumpkin Carrot Cake

Chocolate-Covered Coconut Almond Cake

¾ cup sliced almonds, toasted, divided
1 package (about 18 ounces) yellow cake mix
1 package (4-serving size) vanilla instant pudding and
  pie filling mix
4 eggs
1 cup sour cream
¾ cup water
¼ cup vegetable oil
½ teaspoon coconut extract
½ teaspoon vanilla
⅔ cup shredded coconut, divided
½ cup whipping cream
½ cup semisweet or bittersweet chocolate chips

1. Preheat oven to 350°F. Spray 10- or 12-cup bundt pan with nonstick cooking spray. Coarsely chop ½ cup almonds.

2. Beat cake mix, pudding mix, eggs, sour cream, water, oil, coconut extract and vanilla in large bowl with electric mixer at low speed 30 seconds. Beat at medium speed 2 minutes or until smooth. Fold in chopped almonds and ⅓ cup coconut. Pour batter into prepared pan.

3. Bake 1 hour or until toothpick inserted near center comes out clean. Cool cake in pan 10 to 15 minutes; invert onto wire rack to cool completely.

4. Heat cream in small saucepan just until hot (do not boil). Remove from heat; add chocolate chips and let stand 2 minutes. Whisk until smooth. Let stand at room temperature 15 to 20 minutes or until slightly thickened. Stir; pour glaze over cake. Sprinkle with remaining ¼ cup almonds and ⅓ cup coconut. Refrigerate until ready to serve.   *Makes 12 servings*

Chocolate-Covered Coconut Almond Cake

Creamy Lemon Cake

       2 cups cake flour
       2 teaspoons baking powder
     ¼ teaspoon salt
       1 cup granulated sugar
     ⅔ cup (1⅓ sticks) butter, softened
       4 egg whites, at room temperature
       1 teaspoon vanilla
     ¾ cup buttermilk
    1¼ cups whipping cream
     ½ cup powdered sugar
    1½ teaspoons grated lemon peel
     ¾ cup prepared lemon curd
       Sugared Flowers (recipe follows, optional)

1. Preheat oven to 350°F. Grease two 8-inch round cake pans. Sift flour, baking powder and salt into medium bowl.

2. Beat granulated sugar and butter in large bowl with electric mixer at medium speed until light and creamy. Gradually add egg whites and vanilla; beat at high speed 2 minutes. Reduce speed to low; beat in flour mixture alternately with buttermilk. Pour batter into prepared pans.

3. Bake 23 to 25 minutes or until toothpick inserted into centers comes out clean. Cool cake layers in pans 15 minutes; remove to wire racks to cool completely.

4. Beat cream in medium bowl with electric mixer until thickened. Add powdered sugar and lemon peel; beat until stiff peaks form.

5. Place one cake layer on serving plate; spread with lemon curd. Top with second cake layer; frost top and side of cake with whipped cream mixture. Refrigerate until frosting is set. Garnish with Sugared Flowers before serving, if desired.   *Makes 8 servings*

Sugared Flowers: Brush assorted edible flower petals with 1 pasteurized egg white. Sprinkle generously with granulated sugar; set on wire rack to dry.

Creamy Lemon Cake

Quick Triple Chocolate Cake

1 package (about 18 ounces) chocolate cake mix *without* pudding in the mix
1 package (4-serving size) chocolate instant pudding and pie filling mix
1 cup sour cream
4 eggs
½ cup canola oil
½ cup coffee
1 cup semisweet chocolate chunks or chips
Powdered sugar (optional)
Sweetened whipped cream (optional)

1. Preheat oven to 350°F. Lightly spray nine mini (1-cup) bundt pans or one 12-cup bundt pan with nonstick cooking spray.

2. Beat cake mix, pudding mix, sour cream, eggs, oil and coffee in large bowl with electric mixer at low speed 1 minute. Beat at medium speed 2 minutes or until well blended. Stir in chocolate chunks. Pour batter into prepared pans.

3. Bake 50 to 60 minutes or until toothpick inserted near centers comes out clean. Cool cakes in pans 10 minutes. Loosen cakes from side of pans with small knife, if necessary; invert onto wire racks to cool completely. Sprinkle with powdered sugar and serve with whipped cream, if desired.

Makes 9 cakes

Kitchen Tip

Be sure to wait until the cakes are completely cool before dusting them with powdered sugar (preferably right before serving). If the cakes are still warm, the powdered sugar will dissolve into the cakes and disappear.

Quick Triple Chocolate Cake

Candy Bar Cake

1 package (about 18 ounces) devil's food cake mix *without* pudding in the mix

1 cup sour cream

4 eggs

⅓ cup vegetable oil

¼ cup water

2 containers (16 ounces each) vanilla frosting

1 bar (about 2 ounces) chocolate-covered crispy peanut butter candy, chopped

1 bar (about 2 ounces) chocolate-covered peanut, caramel and nougat candy, chopped

1 bar (about 1½ ounces) chocolate-covered toffee candy, chopped

4 bars (about 1½ ounces each) milk chocolate

1. Preheat oven to 350°F. Grease and flour two 9-inch round cake pans.

2. Beat cake mix, sour cream, eggs, oil and water in large bowl with electric mixer at low speed about 1 minute or until blended. Beat at medium speed 1 to 2 minutes or until smooth. Pour batter into prepared pans.

3. Bake 30 to 35 minutes or until toothpick inserted into centers comes out clean. Cool cake layers in pans 10 minutes; remove to wire racks to cool completely.

4. Cut each cake layer in half horizontally. Place one cake layer on serving plate. Spread generously with frosting. Sprinkle with one chopped candy bar. Repeat with two more cake layers, additional frosting and remaining two chopped candy bars. Top with remaining cake layer; frost top of cake with remaining frosting.

5. Break milk chocolate bars into pieces along score lines. Arrange chocolate pieces around outside edge of cake.   *Makes 12 servings*

Candy Bar Cake

Cupcakes Galore

Triple-Chocolate Cupcakes

1 package (18¼ ounces) chocolate cake mix
1 package (4 ounces) chocolate instant pudding and pie filling mix
1 container (8 ounces) sour cream
4 large eggs
½ cup vegetable oil
½ cup warm water
2 cups (12-ounce package) NESTLÉ® TOLL HOUSE® Semi-Sweet Chocolate Morsels
2 containers (16 ounces *each*) prepared frosting
Assorted candy sprinkles

PREHEAT oven to 350°F. Grease or paper-line 30 muffin cups.

COMBINE cake mix, pudding mix, sour cream, eggs, vegetable oil and water in large mixer bowl; beat on low speed just until blended. Beat on high speed for 2 minutes. Stir in morsels. Pour into prepared muffin cups, filling two-thirds full.

BAKE for 25 to 28 minutes or until wooden pick inserted in centers comes out clean. Cool in pans for 10 minutes; remove to wire racks to cool completely. Frost; decorate with candy sprinkles.

Makes 30 cupcakes

Banana Cupcakes

2 cups all-purpose flour
1½ cups granulated sugar
2 tablespoons packed brown sugar
2 teaspoons baking powder
½ teaspoon salt
½ teaspoon ground cinnamon
¼ teaspoon ground allspice
½ cup vegetable oil
2 eggs
¼ cup milk
1 teaspoon vanilla
2 mashed bananas (about 1 cup)
1 container (16 ounces) prepared chocolate frosting
Chocolate sprinkles (optional)

1. Preheat oven to 350°F. Line 18 standard (2½-inch) muffin cups with paper baking cups.

2. Combine flour, granulated sugar, brown sugar, baking powder, salt, cinnamon and allspice in large bowl. Add oil, eggs, milk and vanilla; beat with electric mixer at medium speed 2 minutes or until well blended. Beat in bananas until well blended. Spoon batter into prepared muffin cups, filling three-fourths full.

3. Bake 25 to 30 minutes or until toothpick inserted into centers comes out clean. Cool cupcakes in pans 10 minutes; remove to wire racks to cool completely.

4. Frost cupcakes; decorate with sprinkles.   *Makes 18 cupcakes*

Banana Cupcakes

Margarita Cupcakes

1 package (about 18 ounces) white cake mix
¾ cup plus 2 tablespoons margarita mix, divided
2 eggs
⅓ cup vegetable oil
¼ cup water
1 tablespoon grated lime peel, divided (3 limes)
   Juice of 1 lime
2 tablespoons tequila or lime juice
3 cups powdered sugar
1 tablespoon sparkling or granulated sugar
1 tablespoon salt (optional)
   Green and yellow food coloring
   Lime peel strips (optional)

1. Preheat oven to 350°F. Line 24 standard (2½-inch) muffin cups with paper baking cups.

2. Combine cake mix, ¾ cup margarita mix, eggs, oil, water, 1 teaspoon lime peel and lime juice in large bowl. Whisk 2 minutes or until well blended. Spoon batter evenly into prepared cups.

3. Bake 20 to 25 minutes or until toothpick inserted into centers comes out clean. Remove cupcakes to wire racks to cool completely.

4. Combine tequila, remaining 2 tablespoons margarita mix and 2 teaspoons lime peel in medium bowl. Gradually whisk in powdered sugar until desired consistency is reached. Combine sparkling sugar and salt, if desired, in small bowl. Add food coloring, one drop at a time, until desired shade of green is reached.

5. Spread glaze over cupcakes; dip edges in sugar-salt mixture. Garnish with lime peel.   *Makes 24 cupcakes*

Margarita Cupcakes

Chocolate Hazelnut Cupcakes

1¾ cups all-purpose flour
1½ teaspoons baking powder
½ teaspoon salt
2 cups chocolate hazelnut spread, divided
⅓ cup (⅔ stick) butter, softened
¾ cup sugar
2 eggs
1 teaspoon vanilla
1¼ cups milk
    Chopped hazelnuts (optional)

1. Preheat oven to 350°F. Line 18 standard (2½-inch) muffin cups with paper or foil baking cups.

2. Combine flour, baking powder and salt in medium bowl. Beat ⅓ cup chocolate hazelnut spread and butter in large bowl with electric mixer at medium speed until smooth. Beat in sugar until well blended. Beat in eggs and vanilla. Add flour mixture alternately with milk, beginning and ending with flour mixture. Spoon batter into prepared muffin cups, filling two-thirds full.

3. Bake 20 to 23 minutes or until cupcakes spring back when touched and toothpick inserted into centers comes out clean. Cool cupcakes in pans 10 minutes; remove to wire racks to cool completely.

4. Frost cupcakes with remaining 1⅔ cups chocolate hazelnut spread. Sprinkle with hazelnuts, if desired.

Makes 18 cupcakes

Kitchen Tip

If the chocolate hazelnut spread is a little stiff and difficult to spread, microwave on LOW (30% power) at 15-second intervals until it softens to a spreadable consistency.

Chocolate Hazelnut Cupcakes

Pink Lemonade Cupcakes

1 package (about 18 ounces) white cake mix *without* pudding
    in the mix
1 cup water
3 egg whites
⅓ cup plus ¼ cup thawed frozen pink lemonade concentrate,
    divided
2 tablespoons vegetable oil
5 to 8 drops red food coloring, divided (optional)
4 cups powdered sugar
⅓ cup (⅔ stick) butter, softened
    Lemon slice candies (optional)

1. Preheat oven to 350°F. Line 24 standard (2½-inch) muffin cups with
paper baking cups.

2. Beat cake mix, water, egg whites, ⅓ cup lemonade concentrate, oil
and 4 to 6 drops food coloring, if desired, in large bowl with electric mixer
at medium speed 2 minutes or until well blended. Spoon batter evenly into
prepared muffin cups.

3. Bake 18 to 22 minutes or until toothpick inserted into centers comes
out clean. Cool cupcakes in pans 5 minutes; remove to wire racks to cool
completely.

4. Beat powdered sugar, butter and remaining ¼ cup lemonade
concentrate in medium bowl with electric mixer at medium speed until
well blended. Beat in remaining food coloring until desired shade of pink
is reached.

5. Spread frosting over cupcakes. Garnish with candies and straws.

Makes 24 cupcakes

Pink Lemonade Cupcakes

Decadent Brownie Cups

1 cup (2 sticks) butter
4 squares (1 ounce each) unsweetened chocolate
2 cups sugar
4 eggs
1 teaspoon vanilla
1 cup all-purpose flour
½ teaspoon salt
20 mini chocolate peanut butter cups

1. Preheat oven to 350°F. Line 20 standard (2½-inch) muffin cups with foil baking cups.

2. Heat butter and chocolate in medium saucepan over very low heat, stirring frequently, until melted and smooth. Remove pan from heat.

3. Gradually stir in sugar until well blended. Add eggs, 1 at a time, mixing well after each addition. Stir in vanilla. Combine flour and salt; stir into chocolate mixture until blended. Spoon into prepared muffin cups, filling about two-thirds full. Place one peanut butter cup in center of each cup.

4. Bake about 18 minutes or until toothpick inserted near centers comes out clean. Serve warm or remove from pans and cool completely on wire racks.   *Makes 20 cupcakes*

Editor's Note

Dense, rich and incredibly delicious, this recipe is an all-time favorite with chocolate lovers. The concept is simple—when you combine brownies and cupcakes, you can't help but have fantastic results!

Decadent Brownie Cups

Cookies & Cream Cupcakes

2¼ cups all-purpose flour
 1 tablespoon baking powder
 ½ teaspoon salt
1⅔ cups sugar
 1 cup milk
 ½ cup (1 stick) butter, softened
 2 teaspoons vanilla
 3 egg whites
 1 cup crushed chocolate sandwich cookies (about 10 cookies),
   plus additional for garnish
 1 container (16 ounces) vanilla frosting

1. Preheat oven to 350°F. Lightly grease 24 standard (2½-inch) muffin cups
or line with paper baking cups.

2. Sift flour, baking powder and salt into large bowl. Stir in sugar. Add
milk, butter and vanilla; beat with electric mixer at low speed 30 seconds.
Beat at medium speed 2 minutes. Add egg whites; beat 2 minutes. Stir
in 1 cup crushed cookies. Spoon batter into prepared muffin cups, filling
two-thirds full.

3. Bake 20 to 25 minutes or until toothpick inserted into centers comes
out clean. Cool cupcakes in pans 10 minutes; remove to wire racks to
cool completely.

4. Frost cupcakes; garnish with additional crushed cookies.

Makes 24 cupcakes

Cookies & Cream Cupcakes

Red Velvet Cupcakes

2¼ cups all-purpose flour
  1 teaspoon salt
  2 bottles (1 ounce each) red food coloring
  3 tablespoons unsweetened cocoa powder
  1 cup buttermilk
  1 teaspoon vanilla
1½ cups sugar
  ½ cup (1 stick) butter, softened
  2 eggs
  1 teaspoon baking soda
  1 teaspoon white vinegar
  1 container (16 ounces) whipped cream cheese frosting
    Toasted coconut (optional)

1. Preheat oven to 350°F. Line 18 standard (2½-inch) muffin cups with paper baking cups.

2. Combine flour and salt in medium bowl. Gradually stir food coloring into cocoa in small bowl until blended and smooth. Combine buttermilk and vanilla in separate bowl.

3. Beat sugar and butter in large bowl with electric mixer at medium speed about 4 minutes or until very light and fluffy. Add eggs, 1 at a time, beating well after each addition. Add cocoa mixture; beat until well blended and uniform in color. Add flour mixture alternately with buttermilk mixture, beating just until blended. Combine baking soda and vinegar in small bowl; gently fold into batter with spatula or spoon (do not use mixer). Spoon batter into prepared muffin cups, filling two-thirds full.

4. Bake 18 to 20 minutes or until toothpick inserted into centers comes out clean. Cool cupcakes in pans 10 minutes; remove to wire racks to cool completely.

5. Generously spread frosting over cupcakes. Sprinkle with coconut, if desired.

Makes 18 cupcakes

Red Velvet Cupcakes

Pumpkin Spice Cupcakes

1½ cups sugar
¾ cup (1½ sticks) butter, softened
3 eggs
1 can (15 ounces) solid-pack pumpkin
1 cup buttermilk
3 cups all-purpose flour
1 tablespoon baking powder
2 teaspoons ground cinnamon
1½ teaspoons baking soda
½ teaspoon salt
¼ teaspoon ground allspice
¼ teaspoon ground nutmeg
⅛ teaspoon ground ginger
Maple Frosting (recipe follows)
Colored decors or sugar (optional)

1. Preheat oven to 350°F. Line 24 standard (2½-inch) muffin cups with paper baking cups.

2. Beat sugar and butter in large bowl with electric mixer at medium speed 3 minutes or until light and fluffy. Add eggs, 1 at a time, beating well after each addition. Combine pumpkin and buttermilk in medium bowl. Combine flour, baking powder, cinnamon, baking soda, salt, allspice, nutmeg and ginger in separate medium bowl. Alternately add flour mixture and pumpkin mixture to butter mixture, beating well after each addition. Spoon batter into prepared muffin cups, filling two-thirds full.

3. Bake 20 to 22 minutes or until toothpick inserted into centers comes out clean. Cool cupcakes in pans 15 minutes; remove to wire racks to cool completely.

4. Prepare Maple Frosting; pipe or spread over cupcakes. Garnish with decors or sugar. *Makes 24 cupcakes*

Maple Frosting: Beat ¾ cup (1½ sticks) softened butter until light and fluffy. Add 3 tablespoons maple syrup and ½ teaspoon vanilla; beat until well blended. Gradually beat in 3½ cups powdered sugar until light and fluffy. Add milk, if necessary, to reach desired spreading consistency.

Pumpkin Spice Cupcakes

1ˢᵗ Birthday Cupcakes

1⅔ cups all-purpose flour
1½ cups sugar
 ½ cup HERSHEY'S Cocoa
1½ teaspoons baking soda
 1 teaspoon salt
 ½ teaspoon baking powder
 2 eggs
 ½ cup shortening
1½ cups buttermilk or sour milk*
 1 teaspoon vanilla extract
 One-Bowl Buttercream Frosting (recipe follows)

To sour milk: Use 4½ teaspoons white vinegar plus milk to equal 1½ cups.

1. Heat oven to 350°F. Line muffin cups (2½ inches in diameter) with paper bake cups.

2. Stir together flour, sugar, cocoa, baking soda, salt and baking powder in large bowl. Add eggs, shortening, buttermilk and vanilla. Beat on low speed of mixer 1 minute, scraping bowl constantly. Beat on high speed 3 minutes, scraping bowl occasionally. Fill muffin cups ½ full with batter.

3. Bake 18 to 20 minutes or until wooden pick inserted in center comes out clean. Remove from pan to wire rack. Cool completely. Frost with One-Bowl Buttercream Frosting.   *Makes about 2½ dozen cupcakes*

One-Bowl Buttercream Frosting

 6 tablespoons butter or margarine, softened
2⅔ cups powdered sugar
 ½ cup HERSHEY'S Cocoa
 ⅓ cup milk
 1 teaspoon vanilla extract

Beat butter in medium bowl. Add powdered sugar and cocoa alternately with milk and vanilla, beating to spreading consistency (additional milk may be needed).   *Makes about 2 cups frosting*

Strawberry Short Cupcakes

2 cups all-purpose flour
2½ teaspoons baking powder
½ teaspoon salt
1 cup milk
1 teaspoon vanilla
1½ cups plus 3 tablespoons sugar, divided
½ cup (1 stick) butter, softened
3 eggs
1½ cups cold whipping cream
2 quarts fresh strawberries, sliced

1. Preheat oven to 350°F. Spray 18 standard (2½-inch) muffin cups with nonstick cooking spray.

2. Combine flour, baking powder and salt in medium bowl. Combine milk and vanilla in small bowl. Beat 1½ cups sugar and butter in large bowl with electric mixer at medium speed about 3 minutes or until creamy. Add eggs, 1 at a time, beating well after each addition. Add flour mixture alternately with milk mixture, beating until well blended. Spoon batter into prepared muffin cups, filling about three-fourths full.

3. Bake 18 to 20 minutes or until toothpick inserted into centers comes out clean. Cool cupcakes in pans 10 minutes; remove to wire racks to cool completely.

4. Beat cream in large bowl with electric mixer at high speed until soft peaks form. Gradually add remaining 3 tablespoons sugar; beat until stiff peaks form.

5. Cut cupcakes in half crosswise. Top each bottom half with about 2 tablespoons whipped cream and strawberries. Replace top half; top with additional whipped cream and strawberries.   *Makes 18 cupcakes*

Strawberry Short Cupcake

Decadent Cheesecakes

Brownie Chocolate Chip Cheesecake

1 (19.5- or 22-ounce) package fudge brownie mix
3 (8-ounce) packages cream cheese, softened
1 (14-ounce) can EAGLE BRAND® Sweetened Condensed Milk
  (NOT evaporated milk)
3 eggs
2 teaspoons vanilla extract
½ cup miniature semisweet chocolate chips

1. Preheat oven to 350°F. Grease bottom only of 9-inch springform pan. Prepare brownie mix as package directs for chewy brownies. Spread evenly in prepared pan. Bake 35 minutes or until set.

2. In large bowl, beat cream cheese until fluffy. Gradually beat in EAGLE BRAND® until smooth. Add eggs and vanilla; mix well. Stir in chocolate chips. Pour into baked crust.

3. Reduce oven temperature to 300°F. Bake 50 minutes or until set.

4. Cool. Chill thoroughly. Remove side of springform pan. Garnish as desired. Store leftovers covered in refrigerator.

Makes one (9-inch) cheesecake

Note: Chocolate chips may fall to brownie layer during baking.

Prep Time: 20 minutes • **Bake Time:** 1 hour, 25 minutes

Blueberry Swirl Cheesecake

1 cup HONEY MAID® Graham Cracker Crumbs
1 cup plus 3 tablespoons sugar, divided
3 tablespoons butter or margarine, melted
4 packages (8 ounces each) PHILADELPHIA® Cream Cheese, softened
1 teaspoon vanilla
1 cup BREAKSTONE'S® or KNUDSEN® Sour Cream
4 eggs
2 cups fresh or thawed frozen blueberries

PREHEAT oven to 325°F. Mix crumbs, 3 tablespoons of the sugar and butter. Press firmly onto bottom of foil-lined 13×9-inch baking pan. Bake 10 minutes.

BEAT cream cheese, remaining 1 cup sugar and vanilla in large bowl with electric mixer on medium speed until well blended. Add sour cream; mix well. Add eggs, 1 at a time, beating on low speed after each addition just until blended. Pour over crust. Purée blueberries in a blender or food processor. Gently drop spoonfuls of puréed blueberries over batter; cut through batter several times with knife for marble effect.

BAKE 45 minutes or until center is almost set; cool. Cover and refrigerate at least 4 hours before serving. Store leftover cheesecake in refrigerator.

Makes 16 servings

Tip: Substitution: Substitute 1 can (15 ounces) blueberries, well drained, for the 2 cups fresh or frozen blueberries.

Make It Easy: Instead of using a blender, crush the blueberries in a bowl with a fork. Drain before spooning over the cheesecake batter and swirling to marbleize as directed.

Prep Time: 15 minutes plus refrigerating • **Bake Time:** 45 minutes

Blueberry Swirl Cheesecake

Praline Cheesecake with Bourbon Pecan Sauce

20 whole graham crackers (10 ounces), broken into 1-inch pieces
¾ cup (1½ sticks) unsalted butter, cubed
1¾ cups packed dark brown sugar, divided
4 packages (8 ounces each) cream cheese, softened
3 tablespoons maple syrup
3 tablespoons all-purpose flour
⅛ teaspoon salt
5 eggs
2 teaspoons vanilla
Bourbon Pecan Sauce (recipe follows)

1. Preheat oven to 350°F. Combine graham crackers, butter and ½ cup brown sugar in food processor; pulse until crumbs begin to clump together.* Press mixture onto bottom and up side of 10-inch springform pan. Bake 10 minutes.

2. Beat cream cheese, remaining 1¼ cups brown sugar and syrup in large bowl with electric mixer at medium-high speed until smooth. Add flour and salt; mix well. Add eggs and vanilla; beat until blended, scraping down side of bowl occasionally. Pour batter into crust.

3. Bake 55 to 60 minutes or until center of cheesecake is just set and edge is puffed and slightly cracked. Cool completely in pan on wire rack; remove side of pan. Cover and refrigerate overnight. Serve with Bourbon Pecan Sauce. *Makes 12 to 16 servings*

Or place graham crackers in resealable food storage bag and crush with rolling pin. Combine with melted butter and brown sugar. Proceed as directed.

Bourbon Pecan Sauce: Combine ¾ cup packed dark brown sugar, ⅓ cup whipping cream, ¼ cup (½ stick) butter, 3 tablespoons light corn syrup and ¼ teaspoon salt in medium saucepan. Bring to a boil over high heat, whisking until sugar dissolves. Reduce heat to medium; boil 1 minute without stirring. Remove from heat. Stir in 3 tablespoons bourbon, then 1½ cups toasted pecan pieces. Cool, stirring occasionally. Refrigerate until ready to serve; reheat before serving.

Praline Cheesecake with Bourbon Pecan Sauce

Chocolate Vanilla Swirl Cheesecake

20 OREO® Chocolate Sandwich Cookies, crushed (about 2 cups)
3 tablespoons butter, melted
4 packages (8 ounces each) PHILADELPHIA® Cream Cheese, softened
1 cup sugar
1 teaspoon vanilla
1 cup BREAKSTONE'S® or KNUDSEN® Sour Cream
4 eggs
6 squares BAKER'S® Semi-Sweet Baking Chocolate, melted, cooled

PREHEAT oven to 325°F. Line 13×9-inch baking pan with foil, with ends of foil extending over sides of pan. Mix cookie crumbs and butter; press firmly onto bottom of prepared pan. Bake 10 minutes.

BEAT cream cheese, sugar and vanilla in large bowl with electric mixer on medium speed until well blended. Add sour cream; mix well. Add eggs, 1 at a time, beating on low speed after each addition just until blended. Remove 1 cup of the batter; set aside. Stir melted chocolate into remaining batter. Pour chocolate batter over crust; top with spoonfuls of remaining plain batter. Cut through batters with knife several times for swirled effect.

BAKE 40 minutes or until center is almost set. Cool. Refrigerate at least 4 hours or overnight. Use foil handles to lift cheesecake from pan before cutting to serve. Store any leftover cheesecake in refrigerator.

Makes 16 servings

Jazz It Up: Garnish with chocolate curls just before serving. Use a vegetable peeler to shave the side of an additional square of BAKER'S® Semi-Sweet Baking Chocolate and a square of BAKER'S® Premium White Baking Chocolate until desired amount of curls are obtained. Wrap remaining chocolate and store at room temperature for another use.

Prep Time: 15 minutes plus refrigerating • **Bake Time:** 40 minutes

Chocolate Vanilla Swirl Cheesecake

Shortbread-Crusted Cheesecake with Raspberry-Ginger Sauce

1 package (10 ounces) shortbread cookies
6 tablespoons butter, cubed, softened
⅓ cup packed light brown sugar
4 packages (8 ounces each) cream cheese, cubed, softened
1 cup granulated sugar, divided
⅛ teaspoon salt
5 eggs
2 teaspoons vanilla
1 package (12 ounces) frozen unsweetened raspberries, thawed
1 teaspoon cornstarch
½ teaspoon grated fresh ginger

1. Preheat oven to 350°F. Place cookies in food processor; process with on/off pulses to break up cookies. Add brown sugar; pulse to form crumbs. Add butter; pulse until mixture begins to stick together.

2. Press crumb mixture onto bottom and 1 inch up side of 9-inch springform pan. Bake 11 minutes or until lightly browned. Cool slightly on wire rack.

3. Place cream cheese, ¾ cup granulated sugar and salt in food processor; process until smooth. Add eggs and vanilla; process until well blended. Pour over crust.

4. Bake 1 hour or until center is almost set and knife inserted 2 inches from edge comes out clean. Cool cheesecake completely in pan on wire rack. Cover loosely with foil and refrigerate overnight.

5. Strain raspberries into small bowl with fine-mesh sieve. Use back of spoon to press raspberries and release as much juice as possible. Discard mashed berries in sieve. Pour juice into measuring cup; add enough water to equal 1 cup liquid. Place in small saucepan with remaining ¼ cup granulated sugar and cornstarch; whisk until cornstarch is completely dissolved. Bring to boil over medium-high heat; boil 1 minute, stirring frequently. Let sauce cool; refrigerate until ready to serve. Stir in ginger just before serving. Serve with cheesecake.   *Makes 12 servings*

Shortbread-Crusted Cheesecake with Raspberry-Ginger Sauce

White Chocolate-Candy Cane Cheesecake

1 cup HONEY MAID® Graham Cracker Crumbs
¾ cup plus 3 tablespoons sugar, divided
3 tablespoons butter, melted
3 packages (8 ounces each) PHILADELPHIA® Cream Cheese, softened
3 eggs
4 squares BAKER'S® Premium White Baking Chocolate, melted
¼ teaspoon peppermint extract
2 cups thawed COOL WHIP® Whipped Topping
½ cup chopped candy canes

PREHEAT oven to 325°F if using a silver 9-inch springform pan (or to 300°F if using dark nonstick 9-inch springform pan). Mix graham crumbs, 3 tablespoons of the sugar and butter; press onto bottom of pan. Bake 10 minutes.

BEAT cream cheese and remaining ¾ cup sugar with electric mixer until well blended. Add eggs, 1 at a time, mixing on low speed after each addition just until blended. Stir in chocolate and extract; pour over crust.

BAKE 45 to 50 minutes or until center is almost set. Run knife or metal spatula around rim of pan to loosen cake; cool before removing rim. Refrigerate at least 4 hours. Top with the whipped topping and chopped candy just before serving. Store leftovers in refrigerator.

Makes 12 servings

How to soften cream cheese: Place completely unwrapped packages of cream cheese in microwavable bowl. Microwave on High 30 to 45 seconds or until slightly softened.

White Chocolate-Candy Cane Cheesecake

Pumpkin Cheesecake with Gingersnap-Pecan Crust

1¼ cups gingersnap cookie crumbs (about 24 cookies)
⅓ cup pecans, very finely chopped
¼ cup granulated sugar
¼ cup (½ stick) butter, melted
3 packages (8 ounces each) cream cheese, softened
1 cup packed light brown sugar
1 teaspoon cinnamon
½ teaspoon ground ginger
¼ teaspoon ground nutmeg
2 eggs
2 egg yolks
1 cup solid-pack pumpkin

1. Preheat oven to 350°F. For crust, combine cookie crumbs, pecans, granulated sugar and butter in medium bowl; mix well. Press crumb mixture evenly onto bottom of ungreased 9-inch springform pan. Bake 10 minutes.

2. Beat cream cheese in large bowl with electric mixer at medium speed until fluffy. Add brown sugar, cinnamon, ginger and nutmeg; beat until well blended. Beat in eggs and egg yolks, 1 at a time, beating well after each addition. Beat in pumpkin until blended. Pour mixture into crust.

3. Bake 1 hour or until edges are set but center is still moist. Turn off oven; let cheesecake stand in oven with door ajar 30 minutes. Transfer to wire rack. Loosen edge of cheesecake from rim of pan with thin metal spatula; cool completely in pan on wire rack.

4. Cover; refrigerate at least 24 hours or up to 48 hours before serving.

Makes 10 to 12 servings

Tip: To help prevent the cheesecake from cracking while baking, place a pan of water in the oven to create moist heat.

Pumpkin Cheesecake with Gingersnap-Pecan Crust

Espresso Chocolate Cheesecake

1 package (10¼ ounces) fudge brownie mix
¼ cup vegetable or canola oil
¼ cup water
4 eggs, divided
1 cup (6 ounces) semisweet chocolate chips
⅓ cup whipping cream
1 to 2 tablespoons instant coffee granules
3 packages (8 ounces each) cream cheese, softened
¼ cup (½ stick) unsalted butter, softened
1 cup sugar
3 eggs
1 teaspoon vanilla
1 jar (10 ounces) raspberry fruit spread
  Whipped cream and raspberries (optional)

1. Preheat oven to 350°F. Grease 9-inch springform pan.

2. Combine brownie mix, oil, water and 1 egg in medium bowl; mix well. Pour batter into prepared pan. Bake 20 minutes or until toothpick inserted 2 inches from edge comes out clean. Cool in pan on wire rack.

3. Heat chocolate chips, cream and coffee granules in small heavy saucepan over medium-low heat until melted and smooth, stirring frequently. Remove from heat; let stand 10 to 15 minutes to cool.

4. Beat cream cheese and butter in large bowl with electric mixer at medium-high speed until smooth. Add sugar; beat until light and fluffy. Add remaining 3 eggs, 1 at a time, beating well after each addition. Add vanilla and melted chocolate mixture; beat at low speed just until blended.

5. Place fruit spread in small microwavable bowl. Microwave on HIGH 30 seconds; stir. Pour melted spread evenly over crust. Pour cheesecake batter over fruit spread.

6. Bake about 40 minutes or until edges are set but center is still moist. Cool to room temperature; cover and refrigerate 24 hours. Let stand 30 minutes at room temperature before serving. Serve with whipped cream and raspberries, if desired. *Makes 10 to 12 servings*

Espresso Chocolate Cheesecake

New York Cheesecake

1 cup crushed HONEY MAID® Honey Grahams (about 6 grahams)
1 cup plus 3 tablespoons sugar, divided
3 tablespoons butter or margarine, melted
5 packages (8 ounces each) PHILADEPHIA® Cream Cheese, softened
3 tablespoons flour
1 tablespoon vanilla
1 cup BREAKSTONE'S® or KNUDSEN® Sour Cream
4 eggs
1 can (21 ounces) cherry pie filling

PREHEAT oven to 325°F. Mix crumbs, 3 tablespoons sugar and butter; press firmly onto bottom of 13×9-inch baking pan. Bake 10 minutes.

BEAT cream cheese, remaining 1 cup sugar, flour and vanilla with electric mixer on medium speed until well blended. Add sour cream; mix well. Add eggs, 1 at a time, mixing on low speed after each addition just until blended. Pour over crust.

BAKE 40 minutes or until center is almost set. Cool completely. Refrigerate at least 4 hours or overnight. Top with pie filling before serving. Store leftover cheesecake in refrigerator. *Makes 16 servings*

Jazz It Up: Omit pie filling. Arrange 2 cups mixed berries on top of chilled cheesecake. Brush with 2 tablespoons melted strawberry jelly.

Editor's Note

This recipe just can't be beat—it's the classic, super-rich, super-dense cheesecake everyone loves and no one can resist. Plus, the 13×9-inch pan makes it extra easy to make and serve.

New York Cheesecake

The publisher would like to thank the companies and organizations listed below for the use of their recipes and photographs in this publication.

Duncan Hines® and Moist Deluxe® are registered trademarks of Pinnacle Foods Corp.

EAGLE BRAND®

Grandma's®, A Division of B&G Foods, Inc.

The Hershey Company

©2009 Kraft Foods, KRAFT, KRAFT Hexagon Logo, PHILADELPHIA AND PHILADELPHIA Logo are registered trademarks of Kraft Foods Holdings, Inc. All rights reserved.

Nestlé USA

VOLUME MEASUREMENTS (dry)

$^1/_8$ teaspoon = 0.5 mL
$^1/_4$ teaspoon = 1 mL
$^1/_2$ teaspoon = 2 mL
$^3/_4$ teaspoon = 4 mL
1 teaspoon = 5 mL
1 tablespoon = 15 mL
2 tablespoons = 30 mL
$^1/_4$ cup = 60 mL
$^1/_3$ cup = 75 mL
$^1/_2$ cup = 125 mL
$^2/_3$ cup = 150 mL
$^3/_4$ cup = 175 mL
1 cup = 250 mL
2 cups = 1 pint = 500 mL
3 cups = 750 mL
4 cups = 1 quart = 1 L

VOLUME MEASUREMENTS (fluid)

1 fluid ounce (2 tablespoons) = 30 mL
4 fluid ounces ($^1/_2$ cup) = 125 mL
8 fluid ounces (1 cup) = 250 mL
12 fluid ounces ($1^1/_2$ cups) = 375 mL
16 fluid ounces (2 cups) = 500 mL

WEIGHTS (mass)

$^1/_2$ ounce = 15 g
1 ounce = 30 g
3 ounces = 90 g
4 ounces = 120 g
8 ounces = 225 g
10 ounces = 285 g
12 ounces = 360 g
16 ounces = 1 pound = 450 g

DIMENSIONS

$^1/_{16}$ inch = 2 mm
$^1/_8$ inch = 3 mm
$^1/_4$ inch = 6 mm
$^1/_2$ inch = 1.5 cm
$^3/_4$ inch = 2 cm
1 inch = 2.5 cm

OVEN TEMPERATURES

250°F = 120°C
275°F = 140°C
300°F = 150°C
325°F = 160°C
350°F = 180°C
375°F = 190°C
400°F = 200°C
425°F = 220°C
450°F = 230°C

BAKING PAN SIZES

Utensil	Size in Inches/Quarts	Metric Volume	Size in Centimeters
Baking or	$8 \times 8 \times 2$	2 L	$20 \times 20 \times 5$
Cake Pan	$9 \times 9 \times 2$	2.5 L	$23 \times 23 \times 5$
(square or	$12 \times 8 \times 2$	3 L	$30 \times 20 \times 5$
rectangular)	$13 \times 9 \times 2$	3.5 L	$33 \times 23 \times 5$
Loaf Pan	$8 \times 4 \times 3$	1.5 L	$20 \times 10 \times 7$
	$9 \times 5 \times 3$	2 L	$23 \times 13 \times 7$
Round Layer	$8 \times 1^1/_2$	1.2 L	20×4
Cake Pan	$9 \times 1^1/_2$	1.5 L	23×4
Pie Plate	$8 \times 1^1/_4$	750 mL	20×3
	$9 \times 1^1/_4$	1 L	23×3
Baking Dish	1 quart	1 L	—
or Casserole	$1^1/_2$ quart	1.5 L	—
	2 quart	2 L	—